T0150440

THE
LITTLE
BOOK
OF
CARMARTHENSHIRE

DR RUSSELL GRIGG

The
History
Press

First published 2015
This paperback edition published 2022

The History Press
97 St George's Place, Cheltenham,
Gloucestershire, GL50 3QB
www.thehistorypress.co.uk

© Dr Russell Grigg, 2015, 2022

The right of Dr Russell Grigg to be identified as the Author
of this work has been asserted in accordance with the
Copyright, Designs and Patents Act 1988.

All rights reserved. No part of this book may be reprinted
or reproduced or utilised in any form or by any electronic,
mechanical or other means, now known or hereafter invented,
including photocopying and recording, or in any information
storage or retrieval system, without the permission in writing
from the Publishers.

British Library Cataloguing in Publication Data.
A catalogue record for this book is available from the British Library.

ISBN 978 0 7509 9873 4

Typesetting and origination by The History Press
Printed and bound in Great Britain by TJ Books Limited, Padstow, Cornwall.

CONTENTS

ACKNOWLEDGEMENTS

I am grateful to Lesley Rees, Policy Research and Information Officer at Carmarthenshire Council, for answering my queries so promptly. The following have also been very supportive: Lyn John and John Wynne Hopkins of Llanelli Community Heritage, and Kathryn Edwards and staff at Llanelli Reference Library. Tom, Mia, Helen, Grace and Sofie have all shown remarkable patience in listening to my stories and trudging around parts of Carmarthenshire. Many thanks to Ruth Boyes (editor of the original edition), Ele Craker and colleagues at The History Press for their editorial support.

All uncredited images form part of The History Press collection.

INTRODUCTION

There are many very good reasons to live in, and visit, Carmarthenshire. To begin with, the county boasts a landscape to retain the interest of most people – stunning beaches, dramatic coastline, ancient woodlands, meandering rivers, atmospheric valleys, lakes and hills, bustling market towns and peaceful villages.

Carmarthenshire or, to give its Welsh name, *Sir Caerfyrddin* (usually shortened to *Sir Gaer*), is a county full of contrasts. The mainly flat coastline runs from just east of Llanelli, beyond Dylan Thomas' village of Laugharne, to Pendine. The Millennium Coastal Park extends for about 10 miles along the Burry Estuary between Llanelli and Burry Port. It offers excellent views of the Gower Peninsula, the UK's first designated area of outstanding natural beauty. The Coastal Park includes the National Wetlands Centre for Wales, a championship golf course and the harbours of Burry Port and Pembrey.

In contrast, the north of the county includes the uplands of the Cambrian Mountains, which run through Mid Wales, described by writers in previous centuries as 'the Green Desert of Wales'. The ancient woodland of Brechfa Forest lies to the north-east of Carmarthen town. Its natural resources have provided a refuge for the Welsh hiding from the Normans, supplied timber for the trenches of the First World War and, in more recent times, proved a popular location for cyclists. To the east of the county lies the Black Mountain, which is in fact a mountain range that straddles the border with Powys. It includes Picws Du (Black Peak), Carmarthenshire's highest point at around 2,000ft, offering spectacular views of the Brecon Beacons National Park.

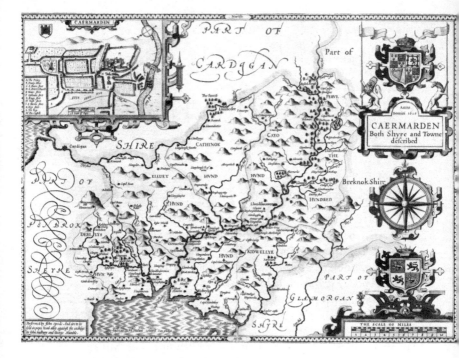

John Speed's 1612 county map, courtesy of Llanelli Library
(Brodie Collection)

The county's main rivers are the Tywi (Towy) and Teifi, seen
clearly on one of the earliest maps of the county, produced by
John Speed in 1612. The Tywi flows south from the Cambrian
Mountains into Carmarthen Bay, where the smaller Taf and
Gwendraeth rivers join it. The Teifi flows west to east from the
Cambrian Mountains along the county's northern border.

For centuries, farming has been a major part of Carmarthenshire's
economy. The most fertile farmland is to be found in the Tywi
Valley, which runs from the east across Carmarthenshire. This is
why settlements began at Llandovery, Llangadog, Llandeilo
and Carmarthen.

The journey through the Carmarthenshire countryside on the
Heart of Wales railway line (Swansea to Shrewsbury) is simply
breathtaking – one of the highlights is to gaze out over the
Cynghordy Viaduct, near Llandovery, 102ft above the valley.

There are equally spectacular views over the Tywi Estuary when travelling along the coastal line from Swansea to Carmarthen.

Carmarthenshire's varied landscape is ideal for a wide range of adventurous activities including rambling, cycling, sailing, abseiling, kayaking, white water rafting, horse riding, gorge walking, caving, canoeing and 'coasteering' (squeezing into a wetsuit and buoyancy aid, and floating around the coast).

The county's wildlife is also one of its selling points: from the possibility of glimpsing red squirrels in the upper Tywi Valley, or standing in awe as salmon leap Cenarth Falls, to feeding red kites at Llanddeusant. Carmarthenshire has thirteen nature reserves managed by the Wildlife Trust of South and West Wales. These include the 63-acre Castle Woods (Dinefwr) near Llandeilo, home to fallow deer and a wide range of birdlife: greater spotted, lesser spotted and green woodpeckers, nuthatches, redstarts, flycatchers, hawks, tawny owls, and roosting wildfowl such as goosander, teal and tufted duck.

Another attraction is the county's rich history, including prehistoric stones erected before the Egyptian pyramids, Iron Age hill forts, medieval abbeys at Talley and Whitland, some of Wales' most dramatic castles, the country's finest Georgian townhouse and the legacy of the coal mining and tinplate industries that once put towns like Llanelli on the world stage.

Carmarthenshire's greatest asset, though, is its people. As Daniel Defoe, author of *Robinson Crusoe*, put it in 1724:

> We found the people of this county more civiliz'd and more curteous, than in the more mountainous parts, where the disposition of the inhabitants seems to be rough, like the country: But here as they seem to converse with the rest of the world, by their commerce, so they are more conversible than their neighbours.

It is in their genetic code for Carmarthenshire people to be resilient, talkative and sociable.

1

CARMARTHENSHIRE: DID YOU KNOW?

Carmarthen is the oldest town in Wales. The Romans built a fort in the town as the regional capital in about AD 75 at the westernmost part of their empire. They built another fort at Caerwent, near Chepstow, at the same time to control south-east Wales. Although Caerwent has some of the best-preserved Roman city walls in Europe, it is now a small village. So Carmarthen is the oldest continuously occupied town in Wales.

A view of Carmarthen

A landmark in the history of women's rights was reached at Whitland in around AD 945. The tenth-century Laws of Hywel Dda were the first in the world to formally declare that a woman was free and not her husband's property. Divorce was permitted by common consent, and in cases of rape, priority was always given to the woman's claims.

The oldest book in the Welsh language was printed in Carmarthen in around AD 1200. *The Black Book of Carmarthen* was named after the colour of its binding and its association with the Black Canons of the Priory of St John the Evangelist. It is thought to be the work of a thirteenth-century Welsh scribe writing at different periods of his life. It is the earliest surviving manuscript written solely in the Welsh language. It covers a mix of poetry, mythology, history, nature and religion, including chants such as:

The first word I will say
When I arise at break of day
'The Cross of Christ be my array'.

The manuscript has been digitised and is now available online at the National Library of Wales website (www.llgc.org.uk/ collections). It is so fragile that a special book cradle had to be used to hold it for photographs to be taken.

A Mayor of Carmarthen killed the last King of England to die on a battlefield in 1485. Sir Rhys ap Thomas was one of the most important men in Tudor Wales. He was Mayor of Carmarthen in 1488–89, one of many privileges he enjoyed following his support in putting Henry Tudor upon the throne of England. But it could have turned out very differently. Rhys had initially sworn loyalty to Richard III, but changed sides for a better offer. Some accounts say that, in the heat of battle at Bosworth Field in 1485, Rhys sought out Richard and struck the fatal blow to the back of the king's head using a halberd (a long-poled axe). In 2012, Richard III's skeleton was found under a car park in Leicester.

The crown handed to Henry Tudor at Bosworth

It took two years of legal dispute before the courts decided that the body should be interred in Leicester Cathedral.

The earliest recorded black resident in the county was an African named Jack of St Christopher. He had been living as a slave in St Kitts in the West Indies before coming to Carmarthenshire. In 1723, he was baptised as an adult in Pembrey and was 'owned' by Lawford Cole who lived in Stradey. There is no record of Jack getting married or having children. He died in 1738 and is burial is recorded in Pembrey.

The first industrial canal in Wales was cut in Carmarthenshire in 1768. Before the coming of the railways in the 1840s, travel by water was quicker and more convenient than by road. Thomas Kymer, a native of Haverfordwest, became Mayor of Kidwelly and was one of the first to exploit the mineral wealth of the Gwendraeth Valley. His 3-mile canal was built between 1766 and 1768. His canal barges carried coal from local pits to the Kidwelly coast for almost thirty years before the dock and river suffered from silting. Facing serious competition from the railways, Kymer's canal was dredged in 1858. A decade later, the canal itself was transformed into the Burry Port and Gwendraeth Valley railway. It connected Burry Port to the pit at Cwmmawr, running through the villages of Trimsaran, Glyn Abbey, Pontyates and Pontyberem. The best place to see the remains of this historic canal is at Kidwelly, beyond the railway station.

Carmarthenshire has the oldest tramroad bridge in Wales and one of the oldest in the world. At Pwll-y-Llygod a tramroad bridge was built in about 1769 to cross the River Gwendraeth Fawr, adjacent to Kymer's canal. It marked the canal's terminus and the tramroad carried anthracite coal from the nearby Carway Colliery to the railway.

The sports historian Martin Johnes suggests that the earliest recorded cricket match to have taken place in Wales was in 1783 on Court Henry Down, Dryslwyn. The two sides were made up of local gentry and clergymen.

A Carmarthenshire man invented the ball bearing in 1794. The idea behind ball bearings is very simple – things move better when

they slide. Although roller bearings were known in ancient times, the first modern recorded patent on ball bearings was awarded in 1794 to Philip Vaughan, a Carmarthen inventor and ironmaster. His design enabled loads to be carried on axles for light and heavy wheel carriages. Today the humble ball bearing is essential to the working of everything from the motor car to aeroplanes, computers to machine tools, and from DVD players to refrigerators.

Britain's first drink-driving warning was issued near Llandovery in 1841. In the lead up to Christmas 1835, a stagecoach driver called Edward Jenkins was drunk while driving the Gloucester to Carmarthen mail coach along the Brecon–Llandovery stretch of the A40 trunk road. Three of his passengers hung on to the stagecoach roof as it veered on to the wrong side of the road, where it met an oncoming cart. The coach plunged off the road over a 121ft precipice and into the river below. The year 1841 saw the Royal Mail erect an obelisk to warn of the dangers of driving whilst intoxicated. The warning is still visible on the roadside.

South Wales and Monmouthshire Training College, 1848

The last cavalry charge on British soil was in Carmarthen. In 1843, protesters known as Rebecca rioters (see Chapter 3) marched up Waterloo Terrace in Carmarthen to attack the workhouse, but they were intercepted by the dragoons. There were no fatalities, but sixty protesters were arrested. In 2014, Carmarthenshire's Regeneration Trust was granted funding to undertake a feasibility study for options on the sustainable use of the gatehouse, the oldest surviving part of the building.

The oldest surviving teacher training college in Wales opened in Carmarthen. The South Wales and Monmouthshire Training College opened its doors to twenty-two male students in 1848 to train them to become teachers in elementary schools. Those admitted were expected to be morally upstanding and physically fit churchmen who had sound literacy skills, including the ability to take notes. In 1931, the governors changed the name to Trinity College to reflect its Church foundation. More recently it has become the University of Wales Trinity Saint David. Women were not admitted until 1957 – one of the reasons for the delay was the fear that they might distract the men from their studies. Even talking to female kitchen staff, without permission, on campus in the 1920s incurred a fine.

Llanelli was once the tinplate capital of the world. From the late eighteenth century and for nearly 200 years, tall chimney stacks of steel, copper and tinworks dominated the Loughor Estuary skyline. At one time, half the world's supply of tinplate came from Llanelli, which was dubbed 'Tinopolis' and 'Sospan' (as saucepans were one of its major supplies). Incidentally, the Welsh name Llanelli was officially adopted in 1966 to replace the Anglicised version of Llanelly. However, both forms lingered on for some years and the old form is retained in Llanelly House.

During the 1920s, Pendine Sands became world famous for land speed records. The 6 miles of Pendine Sands along Carmarthen Bay witnessed enthralling contests between the world's two leading speedsters in the 1920s. In 1924, Sir Malcolm Campbell first set the land speed record of 146mph driving his V12 Sunbeam, one of his famous *Bluebirds*. In 1925 he then exceeded the 150mph barrier, and by 1926 he had reached 174.8mph.

His main rival was John Parry-Thomas, an engineer from Wrexham. In 1927, he took to the sands in a 27,000-litre car he had acquired from his friend Count Zborowski, who had been killed in a Grand Prix. Incidentally, Zborowski's cars were known as Chitty Bang Bangs after the noise emitted from the exhaust pipes. One of these cars inspired Ian Fleming's book of the same name and, later, the musical.

On 3 March 1927, Parry-Thomas tried to beat the world land speed record in the car he had renamed 'Babs'. Sadly he lost control of the car and was killed instantly. Following the inquest into Thomas' death, 'Babs' was buried in the sand dunes. It was excavated and restored in the 1960s and is now on view at the Pendine Museum of Speed. Parry-Thomas was the first driver to be killed in pursuit of the land speed record.

The first canned beer in the United Kingdom was produced at Llanelli in 1935. The Felinfoel brewery was founded around 1835 and, along with Buckley's brewery, became the first to use beer cans, which were manufactured in the 1930s. Crates of Felinfoel were sent out to the Welsh troops during the Second World War. The invention of the beer can brought ale to the masses and changed the way people drink. Nowadays instead of having to go to the pub for a pint, people can call in at a supermarket or off-licence. But, as the Campaign for Real Ale supporters point out, beer cans have not replaced the taste or joys of drinking draught beer.

During the Second World War, a German super fighter nicknamed the 'Butcher Bird' was captured at Pembrey. On 23 June 1942 Armin Faber, an Austrian pilot, was caught up in a dogfight with British Spitfires. Flying a state-of-the-art German Focke-Wulf 190, he mistook the Bristol Channel for the English Channel and landed at RAF Pembrey with very little fuel. He failed to blow up the plane and the RAF gained a valuable asset, sparing the need for a commando raid to capture one in France. The RAF could test and analyse the one German fighter that could outperform the Spitfire.

A Carmarthenshire castle was used in the opening shots of *Monty Python and the Holy Grail* in 1975. Kidwelly Castle appears in the opening scene of Monty Python's historical romp as part of the backdrop for King Arthur and Patsy's retreat.

The National Botanic Garden of Wales, which opened in 2000, has the largest single span glasshouse in the world. The National Botanic Garden was designed by one of the world's leading architects, Norman Foster, and has an area of 568 acres. The exotic plants (960 species) are drawn from six areas of the world: California, Australia, the Canary Islands, Chile, South Africa and the Mediterranean Basin. The Great Glasshouse has a zone for each so that the plants flourish. Kathryn Gustaffson, the architect of the Diana Memorial in Kensington Park, designed the interior landscape of rocky terraces, sandstone cliffs and gravelled scree slopes. It covers almost 1 acre.

It is claimed that the tombs of George III's secret relatives were discovered in St Peter's church, Carmarthen, in 2000. It was always something of a mystery why King George III donated a magnificent pipe organ to St Peter's. However, the answer may have been uncovered by the discovery of hidden tombs under the floorboards. One is dated 1832 and engraved with the

George III

name Charlotte Dalton. Charlotte's mother, Sarah, married James Dalton, a Carmarthen man, although church records do not say where she was buried in the town. Sarah was one of three children from the secret marriage of the Prince of Wales to a young Quaker girl, Hannah Lightfoot. The marriage in 1759 and the subsequent birth of three children were kept secret so that the Prince of Wales could marry someone within his social circle, Princess Charlotte of Mecklenburg-Strelitz. Another tomb is said to belong to 9-year-old Margaret Prytherch, Charlotte's niece, who died in 1839. The discoveries have attracted publicity. However, in the absence of DNA analysis, a sceptical Jeremy Paxman, in his book *On Royalty: A Very Polite Inquiry Into Some Strangely Related Families*, dismisses the tale as one of romantic fiction.

In May 2014, a giant *Dr Who*-style jellyfish was found on Ferryside Sands. The giant barrel jellyfish can grow up to 3.5ft wide and can cause serious injury by stinging unsuspecting swimmers. The one washed ashore at Ferryside measured more than 2ft.

In 2014, during the centenary of Dylan Thomas' birth, the only known film footage of him was discovered. Dylan Thomas is Wales' greatest poet and writer but prior to 2014, it was not known that any film of him existed. Then Jeff Towns, a leading authority on Thomas, announced that he had found a very brief clip of Thomas, who was an extra in the film *Pandora and the Flying Dutchman*, which was finished on Pendine beach in 1951. As Towns said, 'It couldn't be better. You couldn't script it.'

FACTS AND FIGURES

- **183,777** people lived in Carmarthenshire in 2011 according to the census of that year.
- In 2020, this had increased to **190,000** according to the Annual Population Survey carried out by the Office for National Statistics.

- **2,365sq.km,** the land mass of Carmarthenshire, makes it the third largest county in Wales, with 11.5 per cent of the country's total area.
- **40 per cent** of the population live in villages and scattered communities.
- **70 per cent** of the land area is classified as rural.
- **£190,294** is the average price of a property in the county, as of July 2021 (according to Zoopla).
- Around a third of households (27,576) live in Poverty within the county.

The following facts are based on the Annual Report for Carmarthenshire County Council, 2019-2020:
- **71.5%** of eligible people are in employment (UK average is 75.9%)
- **26.5%** of children are overweight or obese, in line with the Welsh average.
- **95%** of parents are satisfied with their child's primary school (89% Welsh average).
- **76%** of people say they feel safe.
- **51.6%** of people say they have a sense of community (52.2% Welsh average).
- **64.6%** of materials are recycled.
- **37.4%** of the population speak Welsh, although this is based on a sample of 600. The 2011 Census figure was 43.9%.
- **113** people were killed or seriously injured on the roads, the 2nd highest in Wales.
- **10.7** is the average number of sick days per year, with the main causes being stress, mental health and fatigue.

2

HISTORY

When does the story of Carmarthenshire begin? Much depends upon what you want to know. If you are interested in its origins as a distinct geographical and political entity, then this begins some 500 years ago with Henry VIII's reforms known as the Acts of Union (1536 and 1542–43). These brought the Welsh and English together under the same legal system and created thirteen counties, of which Carmarthenshire was the largest. We have records for these events – in other words, they are part of recorded history.

But if you are more interested in when the first signs of life appeared in this area, then the answer lies in the ancient

HENRY VIII

rocks of Llangynog. These contain the fossils of 'jellyfish', reported to be swimming in a shallow sea surrounding large volcanoes up to 570 million years ago. Geologists think that the small jellyfish were stranded, possibly by a receding tide, and later entombed by sediment. So Carmarthenshire's birth certificate is its rocks. In the National Botanic Garden there is a Rock of Ages exhibition – boulders on the walk up from the entrance tell the story of Wales over millions of years.

This time span of *natural* history is difficult to grasp. But imagine a ten-by-ten grid (100 squares) representing the story of Carmarthenshire. You would need to colour in 99.9 of these squares to represent its prehistory – that is, the time before written records existed.

ICE AGE

Much of our 100-square grid would have been covered in ice. But the so-called Ice Age was not a period of continuous ice cover. Rather it was a complex series of cold periods known as 'glacials', spanning at least 2 million years. At times it was so cold (as low as -80°C) that the snow did not melt, even in summer. Over time, the ice layers became thicker and thicker until the whole of Britain was buried under a sheet of ice up to 1.5 miles deep covering Snowdon, Wales' tallest mountain (1,085m). In between these very cold periods there were warmer times (known as 'interglacial'), similar to today's temperatures, when the ice would melt and retreat to higher altitudes.

Up until about 5000 BC, Britain was connected to mainland Europe, which enabled animals and humans to move as the climate changed. Mammoths and woolly rhinos, which thrived in the cold, headed for Britain while warmth-loving creatures, such as hippos and elephants, travelled south in search of a warmer climate and food. There was no such thing as Carmarthen Bay; rather, it would have been a dry plain. Our early ancestors were able to walk from what is now Porthcawl to Mumbles Head, from the Gower to Tenby. Further afield, people and animals could cross the dried-out floor of the English Channel and southern North Sea.

Human prehistory is so long that Christian Thomsen, a nineteenth-century Danish museum curator, came up with the idea of dividing the time into three phases when he arranged the museum's collections for display. He based this on the relative technological challenges the earliest peoples faced in fashioning stone, bronze and iron into weapons and tools. Later, the Stone Age was itself sub-divided to reflect the increasingly sophisticated development of tools (the Greek word for stone is *lithos*):

- Palaeolithic (Old or Early Stone Age), 2.6 million–10000 BC.
- Mesolithic (Middle Stone Age), 10000–5000 BC.
- Neolithic (New Stone Age), 5000–800 BC.

Despite scientific advances, prehistoric dating is a hazy business. The uncertainty is because the landscape was effectively wiped clean by the Ice Age, which disturbed whatever evidence had been left by humans, and carried tools and objects away from where they had been abandoned or dropped.

PALAEOLITHIC BEGINNINGS

If you are interested in Carmarthenshire's *human* origins, then the starting points are its ancient caves. We know that Coygan Cave, near Laugharne, was used as a lookout point for reindeer, bison and horses that roamed the plain that became the Bristol Channel. Unfortunately archaeologists have found no human bones in the cave but, based on evidence from stone axes that were discovered, they think it was occupied briefly anytime between 60,000 and 40,000 years ago. The oldest human remains in Wales were found in Pontnewydd Cave, near St Asaph in Denbighshire, and have been dated to 230,000 years ago. Nineteen human teeth were discovered, belonging to five individuals, including the upper jaw of a child aged around 8 years old.

Since the first discovery in 1848 of a strange skull with ape-like features (distinct brow ridges and forward projecting face) in Gibraltar, the early people have been dubbed 'Neanderthals' – often mocked in popular culture as ugly, primitive grunters but ironically named after a poet and hymn composer called Joachim Neander, who gave his name to a German valley which inspired his work and where prehistoric human remains were later found. Setting aside the literary associations, the *Telegraph* (3 November 2010) confirmed that 'Neanderthals really were sex-obsessed thugs'. This followed scientific analysis of prehistoric bones, which revealed that they were exposed to more testosterone during physical development. From this, scientists concluded that Neanderthals were more likely to have started fights and to have multiple partners.

Unfortunately we have very little evidence for Neanderthals in Carmarthenshire. The three small stone hand axes discovered in Coygan Cave were typical of the weapons used to attack prey. The stone tools available included the multi-purpose axe and sharp knives, as well as scrapers for preparing hides and spears. Animal skins were used for tents, shelters, bedding and clothes. In the Czech Republic, Poland and Ukraine, the remains of Ice Age homes have been found, where mammoth tusks covered with animal skins were used as support structures. Skeletons excavated around Europe show that many Neanderthals suffered a very high number of broken bones, probably inflicted by animals. Coygan Cave was eventually abandoned and taken over by animals as a den. The Coygan findings are online as part of the impressive People's Collection of Wales (www.peoplescollection.wales/items/11775). These include a woolly rhinoceros tibia (leg bone) that has been gnawed by a hyena seeking to extract the marrow. We know that an Iron Age hill fort was established at Coygan, but it was abandoned during the Roman period.

Coygan is not the only Carmarthenshire cave where evidence of early human occupation has been discovered. In 1813, the remains of a dozen skeletons were found at Craig Derwyddon caves near Llandybïe. In each case the skulls rested on a ledge 6in higher than the body. In 1907 an archaeologist found the remains

Carreg Cennen Castle

of two adults and two children in a cave on the site of Carreg Cennen Castle, but these were not considered prehistoric. Also recovered was a horse's incisor tooth, which had a hole drilled in one end, possibly for suspension on a necklace. Sadly many of Carmarthenshire's prehistoric caves, including Coygan, were lost forever following quarrying and mining operations during the nineteenth century.

We do not know why or exactly when the Neanderthals disappeared. At a major conference in 2013, experts argued over whether 'modern' humans (*homo sapiens*) were responsible for a gradual take-over of Neanderthal territories. Another theory blames a devastating volcanic eruption in Naples 39,000 years ago. This produced huge plumes of ash across Europe that blotted out the sun, possibly for years, causing temperatures to plummet.

But Neanderthals are experiencing something of a comeback. A study of fossils and genetic analysis has suggested that Neanderthals and modern humans share many characteristics. Neanderthals made tools, arranged the burial of their loved ones, travelled, explored new areas and worked in teams. To survive as long as they did in the freezer of the Ice Age called for high-level teamwork and problem-solving skills, particularly in hunting and gathering food.

MESOLITHIC MELTDOWN

The time between the end of the last Ice Age and the introduction of farming is known as the Mesolithic period (*c.* 10000–4400 BC). Humans began to use new types of stone tools in the form of long, thin blades made from flint. These were more versatile than the older tools.

From around 10000 BC, the climate grew warmer, ice sheets melted and sea levels began to rise. This was the point at which Britain became an island. In about 6000 BC, a massive tsunami was created following a landslide on the Norwegian coast and the water swept over the land to form the North Sea. In Carmarthenshire, the retreating glaciers carved out the Tywi Valley. Such climatic change was more sudden than in previous times. Cold and dry conditions were replaced by a milder and more humid climate. Cold-loving animals retreated, which robbed Palaeolithic hunters of their main food supply. So their Mesolithic descendants now faced very different living conditions. The spread of forests opened up new food sources in berries, roots and small game, in addition to fishing.

Very little Mesolithic evidence has been found in Carmarthenshire, other than a few flint blades on the Black Mountain. These may have formed part of arrowheads, knives or harpoons to spear fish. During the excavations for a new school (Ysgol Bro Dinefwr in Llandeilo), which opened in 2013, archaeologists found stone flakes and blades which they think were either lost or discarded during the Mesolithic period.

NEOLITHIC REVOLUTION

The word 'revolution' is often over-used when describing the past but it is very fitting to sum up what happened around 6,000 years ago. Put simply, people turned their hand to farming and living in settlements, rather than roaming about reliant upon fishing, hunting and gathering their food. Archaeologists now think it was a bit more complicated than this – they have examined domestic refuse from Coygan, which suggests that the cave was occupied for short periods. In other words, these people were still quite mobile in searching for food although they may have lived alongside other groups who started to settle and farm the land. This took plenty of skill, time and forward planning. Grain had to be stored in pits for the winter. Woodland had to be cleared. About a dozen or so Neolithic stone axes have been found in the county. These are important because they tell us where the people settled, and in nearly all cases this was along the Tywi and Taf rivers. Archaeologists have also found arrowheads and multi-purpose scrapers at Nantgaredig, which are on display at the museum in Abergwili. Dogs and pigs were domesticated from wolves and wild boar.

There was nothing primitive about our Neolithic ancestors. They were skilled farmers and builders. They made a range of stone tools, such as knives, scrapers, boring tools, adzes and arrowheads to kill and skin animals, prepare hides, work wood and leather, and prepare food. From surviving post-holes at Llandegai in North Wales, archaeologists have sketched out what a Neolithic house may have looked like. It was 13m in length and 6m across, divided into three rooms: a big central living room

with a hearth and two smaller rooms, one at each end. One of these was a storeroom with a raised bed for sleeping, the other was an open living space with a central fire.

Imagine the planning skills needed to move huge 45-ton slabs of stone 160 miles east from the Preseli hills in Pembrokeshire to the open plain where Stonehenge now stands. This is what happened 5,000 years ago, and it is rightly considered one of the most extraordinary feats of engineering in the world. We know that the Neolithic people built the first trackway into the marshes of the Somerset Levels. In Carmarthenshire and elsewhere, consider the efforts involved in building the megalithic tombs or cromlechs that still survive – large upright slabs supporting a single capstone. These landmarks testify to the physical strength of Neolithic people. Archaeologists have examined Neolithic bones found in South Wales that show strong muscular attachments. They conclude that they routinely ran and jumped, rather than walked, and pulled bowstrings, which gave them well-developed physique. They did not need to attend the gym.

In 2021 one of the longest archaeological projects (started in 2005) was completed, which followed the route of laying the new South Wales Gas Pipeline. It unearthed deep prehistoric ditches, the remains of a 4,500-year-old Neolithic community at Vaynor Farm, but unfortunately no artefacts were found.

Of the sixteen cromlechs in Carmarthenshire, the best preserved is Gwal-y-filiast ('lair of the greyhound bitch'), in the small village of Llanglydwen near Llanboidy. It is hidden away among trees overlooking the River Taf. Four uprights support the large capstone and originally an oval or circular mound of earth covered the tomb. We are not sure exactly how these monuments were used: aside from places for burial, they may have been gathering places for community events. Carmarthenshire also has numerous Neolithic stone circles and freestanding stones. Again, we do not know why they were built – they may have marked important graves, or they were perhaps phallic symbols related to fertility worship. The Brynmaen Standing Stone, on private farmland in Llannon, is one of the tallest at 3.5m.

A reconstruction of Neolithic man at the National Museum of Wales is based on the oldest skull in Wales, found in Talgarth (Powys) and dates to about 3650 BC. He looks no different to a modern Western man and reminds us that, without our gadgets, we still resemble Stone Age people.

BRONZE AGE

Around 2300 BC, metal objects became more widely available across Europe. Wales had some of the earliest copper mines, for example at Mynydd Parys in Llandudno. But it was bronze, an alloy from tin and copper, which could be shaped into hardened tools and weapons. Metalsmiths became much respected in society, as they produced the axes, spearheads, chisels and other tools essential for survival. Some of these can be seen at the County Museum, found locally by farmers ploughing their fields. In 1938, Pencader farmer Ifor Davies struck a decorated urn, which contained the remains of an adult at least 3,000 years old. Unfortunately, his plough had shattered a second urn.

In the British Museum, as part of the nineteenth-century Meyrick Collection, there is a remarkably preserved Bronze Age shield found in the marsh at Rhyd y Gors, Carmarthen. In 2011 a metal detecting enthusiast found thirteen items buried 3,000 years ago at St Ishmael, Ferryside. The treasure hoard included a bronze bracelet, fragments of a large bronze spearhead and a complete bronze socketed axe. These were likely to be offerings to the gods, buried with a spectacular view across Worm's Head.

The county also has around 100 Bronze Age burial mounds. Recent research at one such site on the Black Mountain suggests that the practice of placing flowers at gravesides dates back at least 4,000 years. In the middle of the mound, archaeologists found a large rectangle stone built cist that had been covered by a large capstone. Inside were the cremated bones of a young child, a pottery urn, a bone pin (to fasten clothes) and several flint tools. By analysing the soil, the archaeologists detected microscopic pollen grains, which suggested that the child's burial was accompanied by a floral tribute of meadowsweet. Amazingly, the same burial rituals, with cremated bone, pottery and meadowsweet flowers in a stone cist, have been found as far away as Orkney and Perthshire in Scotland.

IRON AGE

Around 800 BC iron tools, which were harder and sharper than those made of bronze or wood, were introduced into Wales from the Continent. These tools meant that forests could be cleared more easily and, with the iron plough, the land cultivated more effectively. A wetter climate and poor soil led to competition for land. As a result, some people fortified their dwellings with banks and ditches, while others remained undefended.

The main feature of Iron Age Carmarthenshire, along with the rest of south-west Wales, was the defended enclosure. Large hill forts tended to be built in the northern and eastern parts of the region. Two of the most prominent were located at Garn Goch near Llangadog and in the Tywi Valley at Merlin's Hill, Abergwili. At Garn Goch there are technically two hill forts covering an area of 11 ha (around thirteen football pitches) with walls as high as 6.5m and some 25m wide! Clearly, the chief responsible for its construction would have been a very powerful figure.

There were numerous smaller farmsteads scattered around the county. These tended to be located in low-lying, southern parts such as Penycoed, near Llanddowror. Some sites have no surviving earthworks and the only clues are the Welsh place names such as Dinas Bach and Dinas Fawr in Rhandirmwyn, Mandinam and Llangadog. Unfortunately archaeologists have unearthed relatively few Iron Age artefacts in the county.

So where did these Iron Age people come from? It was once thought that over several centuries they arrived from central Europe. More recently DNA analysis suggests that the Celts (Irish, Scots and Welsh) arrived via the Atlantic coastal route from Ice Age refuges including the Basque country, with the modern languages we call Celtic arriving later. The Greeks called these people the *Keltoi* or Celts. They have left lots of material evidence over many lands, from what is now Spain to Hungary, Austria to Wales. There were strong cultural similarities between the ancient Celts across Europe; for example their artwork, weapons and tools were adorned with the same decorative features, such as leaves, animal shapes and the human head.

Obviously there were also differences between these peoples. The tall blond Celts of central Europe were not the same in physical appearance as the tribesmen in south-east Wales, who the Romans later described as swarthy with curly hair. Genetic maps of the British Isles suggest that the Welsh are the oldest Britons and carry DNA that can be traced back to the last Ice Age, 10,000 years ago.

The Celts were primarily builders, traders, farmers and warriors. Most of the people of Britain, from Cumbria to Cornwall, spoke an early form of Welsh called Brythonic. They wove clothes, reared cattle and sheep, and grew wheat. Evidence from the Iron Age Coygan Camp gives an insight into how the land

was farmed. Archaeologists have analysed animal bones to show that 64 per cent were cattle, with sheep and goats making up 16 per cent, pigs 15 per cent and the rest comprising other animals. At nearby Pen-y-coed (Llangynog), the remains of a simple grain store have been found and there is also evidence for cereal farming on Pembrey Mountain, overlooking Carmarthen Bay. The Celts established a well-deserved reputation as brilliant metalworkers, poets and artists. They enjoyed festivals and storytelling around the central fireplace.

The reconstructed roundhouses at Castell Henllys, near Newport in neighbouring Pembrokeshire, offer further insight into life during the Iron Age. In 2000, the BBC used the site to conduct a televised living history experiment called *Surviving the Iron Age* (a similar thing had been tried in England during the 1970s). Seventeen volunteers left their toothbrushes behind for a seven-week retreat to West Wales. One of their outstanding memories was the feeling of utter exhaustion. Despite certain concessions due to BBC insurance (they collected water from a pipe, for example), the modern-day hippies minded and killed animals, collected firewood, baked bread, lit fires, made clothes out of animal skins and bickered in true soap-opera fashion, the outcome of which was a feeling that the Sweat Age might be a more appropriate label than the Iron Age.

ROMAN CARMARTHENSHIRE

Carmarthenshire was a very long way from the heart of the Roman Empire. It would have taken around eighty days to travel from Rome to Carmarthen in the first century AD. Even for the Roman troops stationed in Gaul (France) or Londinium, the provincial capital, getting to West Wales was not straightforward. Before the Romans came to Wales, there were no roads, just rough tracks. It was to take the best part of thirty years for the Romans to occupy Wales. They never really conquered the land. So why did they bother venturing west at all? Clearly, the weather wasn't an attraction.

On the other hand, the lure of Carmarthenshire gold and other minerals proved a very attractive proposition. Tucked away in the wooded hillsides overlooking the beautiful Cothi Valley is Dolaucothi, the only known Roman gold mine in Britain and a site of international significance. The Romans probably heard about it through traders and arrived in the area by about AD 78. The Romans did not do things in half measures. They built a system of hydraulics whereby water was stored in

tanks cut into the rocks, and then released to remove topsoil, drive machinery and wash crushed ore. They established a base camp in the village of Pumpsaint with a granary, workshops, furnace and bathhouse for a detachment of troops. They set about driving shafts or 'adicts' horizontally into the hillside, building stone aqueducts, one of which was 7 miles in length.

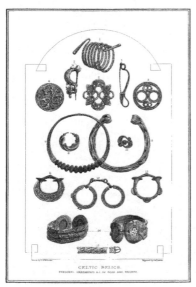

CELTIC RELICS.
PERSONAL ORNAMENTS &c. OF GOLD AND BRONZE.

Miners (slaves) removed around 500,000 tons of rock from the surface. Poignantly, they left their marks on the walls.

Archaeologists have also found snake-shaped bracelets, brooches and other ornaments to show that goldsmiths were busy in the area. We have no idea how many died extracting the gold but it would have been a dangerous business – aside from the risks of rockfalls and collapsing shafts, miners were exposed to protracted lung diseases from breathing in the dust. The human cost of mining minerals has had a long and painful history in Carmarthenshire.

The extracted gold was sent on its long journey by track and sea to the imperial mints, for instance at Lyons. Gold was important to the Romans because it set the value of other things. During the first century AD, a pound of gold was worth forty-five coins. By the fourth century AD, it rose to seventy-two coins, making each coin worth less and the price of gold worth more.

In practice this meant that when middle-class Romans went to the shops, they had less money in their pockets to afford their daily needs – this inflation created tensions and economic anxiety, which contributed to the decline of Rome.

The Romans abandoned the Dolaucothi mine in about AD 140 and it was not reopened until the Victorians used explosives to open up new shafts. The mines finally closed in 1938 and they are now owned by the National Trust, which provides guided tours, an exhibition centre and opportunities to pan for gold in safer circumstances.

ROMAN LEGACY

Perhaps the funniest question in film history was uttered in Monty Python's *Life of Brian* (1979):

Alright, but apart from the sanitation, the medicine, education, wine, public order, irrigation, roads, the fresh-water system, and public health, what have the Romans ever done for us?

So what did the Romans ever do for Carmarthenshire aside from steal its gold or, to put it in a more constructive way, introduce large-scale industry to the region?

The two most significant Roman contributions both nationally and locally were the introduction of Christianity and the Latin language. Unfortunately we do not know much about the mechanics of how Christianity arrived in Carmarthenshire, but it is likely to have been through traders, administrators or soldiers converted to the new faith. Neither do we know much about the transition from paganism to Christianity; although by AD 400, Christianity was the official religion of the Empire. In some cases, ancient pagan beliefs were assimilated into the new religion rather than dismissed. Christmas, for example, is rooted in a pagan winter festival.

The language of the early Church was Latin. It is easy to forget the fact that Latin dominated official business, education and culture for centuries. For example, pupils at Carmarthen Grammar School, Llandovery public school and students at Carmarthen's teacher training college continued to study Latin well into the twentieth century. The Welsh word for school, *ysgol*, is derived from the Latin *schola*. Welsh adopted Latin words in activities such as writing, farming, cooking, building and mining. Around 1,000 Welsh words are derived from Latin. Examples include:

Ffrwyn – frenum (bridle)
Padell – patella (pan)
Ffenestr – fenestra (window)
Aur – aurum (gold)
Llyfr – liber (book)

We have the Romans to thank for our first written references to Carmarthenshire. In about AD 150, a Greco-Roman traveller named Claudius Ptolemy wrote a book called 'Geography'. In it he calls the people who lived in West Wales the *Demetae*, from which we get the modern Dyfed. He then mentions their two towns, *Luentinum* (probably Dolaucothi) and *Maridunum* (Carmarthen). Later in the second century AD in a book about Roman travel, called the *Antonine Itinerary*, a slightly different spelling of what is now Carmarthen appears (*Muridunum*) and is said to be literally 'at the end of the road' – 186 miles from the Roman camp at Wroxeter in Shropshire.

Carmarthen became the first Romano-British town in Wales. This meant that it was the self-governing capital of the *Demetae* tribe. The Romans won over the local tribal leaders by offering new goods and services and a degree of independence in exchange for taxes or tributes. The Romans made full use of the River Tywi to bring in new consumer goods including wine, olive oil, fine pottery, paved floors and exotic jewellery but, rather than build a bridge over the river, they built one in nearby marshland and then redirected the river! The introduction of Roman ways and culture was the most effective means of keeping a sense of order and duty in the region without over-stretching Roman troops. The County Museum includes brooches, glass beads, lamp, coins, pottery and a carved bone knife handle, and a broken gravestone that was found along Priory Street. Given the cost of gravestones, this must have belonged to a high-status citizen. There is a Roman altar in St Peter's church, also found in Priory Street, the oldest street in Carmarthen and once the main thoroughfare in the Roman town.

It is difficult to piece together life in Roman Carmarthen from what survives. But simple things, like the use of a ceramic lamp with a spout to hold the wick for domestic lighting, was an improvement on the tallow candle that gave off an offensive smell and often wilted. The County Museum has two Roman oil lamps, discovered in 2001 by a JCB driver at Johnstown. They were buried within a pot, still showing their maker's name. Lamps were often buried with the dead to provide light for the next world.

To the east of Carmarthen town are the remains of the amphitheatre, one of only seven in Roman Britain and the most westerly. It was lost for the best part of 1,500 years and only came to light in 1944 when a new housing estate was being planned. In its heyday, the amphitheatre played host to games, parades and religious festivals, with a capacity of around 5,000 spectators. This exceeded the town's population, which suggests that it also catered for natives in the surrounding area. Archaeological digs near Priory Street have found foundations of Roman workshops, shops and houses. The town itself was built on the classic Roman 'playing-card' design. It is possible to trace the outline by walking along Richmond Terrace, one side of the town. Roman brick walls were still standing more than 1,000 years later when Giraldus Cambrensis (Gerald of Wales) visited Carmarthen in 1188 while recruiting support for the Crusades.

Elsewhere, we also know that the Romans built a Roman fort at Loughor (*Leucarum*); they probably also built a bridge across the river towards what is now Llanelli. Here, there are some place name clues that hint at the area's distant Roman past – 'Stradey' is a reminder of the *strata* or Roman road, while 'Spitty' is associated with *hospicium* or hospital, for the garrison at Loughor. Early town maps refer to a probable Roman camp called 'Pen-y-Castell' in the area of John Street and Castle buildings.

Roman camp, sketch by John Wynne Hopkins

Archaeologists have also found evidence for Roman forts at Llandovery (near the hamlet of Llanfair-ar-y-bryn) and Llandeilo (within the grounds of Dynevor Park). These linked Carmarthen to Brecon. The Romans also set up marching camps at Y Pigwyn on the summit of Mynydd Bach, Trecastell. Here, some 4,000–5,000 legionaries were expected to put tents up, light fires and be ready for action within hours. These temporary camps were erected all over Britain and were designed to take the fight to the enemy.

Above all, the Romans provided the blueprint for the Welsh road network. In Wales, they built around 750 miles of roads, many of which later formed the basis of the nineteenth-century railways and modern holiday routes. Sarn Helen extends 160 miles from the forts at Neath to Conwy in the north. In Carmarthenshire, it runs through the Cothi and Teifi valleys. The name Sarn Helen refers to Elen, a Romano-British princess and the wife of the Commander of Britain, Magnus Maximus (*c.* 335–338), known as Macsen Wledig in Welsh. Elen is said to have persuaded her husband to build the road. Llandovery sits on a Roman crossroads with links to Trawscoed via Pumsaint and Llanio. East of Llandovery, the Roman road connects to Trecastle via Y Pigwn marching camps and a small fort at Waun Ddu.

The Romans occupied Carmarthenshire for some 350 years. Given that a comparable period of time would take us back to the Great Fire of London, clearly the Romans left their impact on the area even though archaeological findings have been relatively few. The Roman influence, however, was not as great as in the south-east of Wales. In fact, even within Roman Carmarthenshire, influence on everyday life became weaker the further people lived from *Maridunum*. Most people continued to eke out an existence on isolated farms as they had done for generations before the Roman invasion.

The decline of Roman interest in Carmarthenshire is linked to the wider disintegration of the Roman Empire. Barbarian attacks in mainland Europe drew troops away from Britain. The south-east of the country became open to attacks from Angles, Saxons and Jutes from the east, while sea raiders from Ireland pillaged the western coastline. When the Romans finally pulled out of Wales in AD 383, they left a well-organised land. Even the Welsh nationalist politician Gwynfor Evans, elected Member of Parliament for Carmarthenshire in 1966, acknowledged that the Roman Empire 'contributed more to our life than it took out', although he added for good measure 'the British Empire took much more out than it put in'.

THE MIDDLE AGES (410–1485)

The period immediately following the departure of Roman troops from Britain to the coming of the Normans is traditionally called the Dark Ages. This sums up the evidential difficulties historians face in tracing what happened during this time. It is certainly challenging to reconstruct history from a few standing stones, scattered medieval artefacts and a handful of descriptions by monks and poets.

But the Dark Ages label is misleading. Modern Welsh historians offer a far more upbeat analysis of the post-Roman centuries and prefer terms such as the Heroic Age or Early Christian Age. For some, a sense of what it means to be Welsh began when the Romans left – Wales established itself as a distinct territory, Hywel Dda (the Good) brought together enlightened native laws, and Welsh language and culture flourished. In fact, during the seventh century it was possible to travel from Edinburgh to Cornwall speaking Welsh all the way. Place names along the route still show their Welsh origins, such as Melrose (*Moelrhos*), the bare headland, and Ecclefechan (*Eglwys Fechan*), the little church.

The surviving stone evidence shows the influence of the Irish in Carmarthenshire. The stones bear both Latin and the Irish script of Ogham, which is made up of strokes and notches. Ogham takes its name from the legendary Irish god Ogma, who conveyed souls to the 'Otherworld'. The script was thus used for particular purposes, such as funeral memorials, marker stones and for divination, but not generally for poetry. The Irish dynasty of Desi became the most powerful in the area and remained so until the tenth century.

The most famous stone, discovered in 1895, is known as the Voteporix Stone and is kept at the County Museum. It once stood outside the entrance to Castell Dywran churchyard in Clynderwen in the south-west corner of the county. It commemorates Voteporix, a sixth-century ruler of Demetia (Dyfed). He was of Irish descent and was given the Roman title of Protector. There are also early medieval stone memorials at the churches of Llandawke, Llansadurnen and Eglwys Cymmin.

The Development of Christianity in Carmarthenshire

The Age of the Saints (450–700) describes the influence of holy men such as Dewi (David), Teilo and Cadog in the spread of Christianity. The influence of David is illustrated by dedications to him at Bettws, Capel Dewi and Llannon. Christianity has shaped much of the early history of the county and this is best reflected in the place names, customs and surviving buildings. There are fifty-eight churches in the county, of which around a third are said to have medieval origins, indicated by their substantial towers (some up to 70ft). These include the churches at Llansteffan, Llangyndeyrn, Llanddowror and Llanllwni.

The medieval parish churches of Carmarthenshire were not simply places for worship or the performance of the three key rituals of baptism, marriage and burial. Churches were the centres of community life, serving as meeting places, providing relief for the sick and even occasionally brewing ale. This was sold to raise funds and was drunk during church fairs. The churches also stood as a place of refuge against marauders. This might partly explain the thick church walls and small windows.

In medieval Carmarthen, the Augustinian Priory of St John and the Franciscan Friary were the two religious orders that controlled much of the town's everyday life. The priory ruled what was known as the Old Town of perhaps 100 households, and became one of the richest foundations in Wales. It had three mills powered by water from the Gwyli, a tributary of the River Tywi. It is still possible, near Glangwili hospital, to see part of a medieval leat that supplied water to the mills. The only remains of the priory are part of the precinct wall in the south-west corner of Parc Hinds recreation ground in Llangunnor, and the arched entrance of the gatehouse, the rest of which has been converted into four modern houses. In 1979, excavations revealed the footings of the church, chapter house and prior's lodgings, and also uncovered medieval glazed tiles and stained glass.

When walking around the present Wilkinson store in the Greyfriars Centre, it is hard to imagine that this was once the site of the largest recorded British Greyfriary outside London. The friary

was founded around 1270 and comprised a church, chambers, kitchen, brewery and buttery. The Greyfriars (*Y Brodyr Llwyd*) were highly skilled gardeners, herbalists, bakers and cooks who also brewed their own beer. Their name derives from the colour of their hooded tunic or habit. They took a vow of poverty, seeking only opportunities to serve their fellowmen and worship God. Sadly, nothing remains of the building in Carmarthen. The 5-acre site was bounded on the northern side by Lammas Street, on the west by a brook that ran by Heol y Morfa, and on the east by another brook running through what is now Blue Street. Both brooks fed into the River Tywi, which lapped the south side and provided the monks with ample Friday fish. The main entrance was from Lammas Street. A friar's preaching cross was located outside the entrance, in the middle of the street.

One of the most important religious communities in Wales was in Llandeilo, where monks busied themselves in copying religious texts to the extent that it became known as 'the scholar's town' (*Tre'r Ysgolheigion*). Abbey Terrace is a reminder of the time when the Abbots of Talley collected tithes from the people of Llandeilo. There is a lane leading down to the footbridge across the river known as Abbot's Barn (*Ysgubor Abad*) and may refer to where the tithes were stored.

The Church influence can be seen in the many place names beginning with *Llan*, which originally meant an enclosed consecrated area for burial. It is identified with nearly all the names of parish churches in Wales. Llanelli is named after Elli, who was a disciple of St Cadog. According to legend, Cadog was asked by a distressed queen to help her, through prayer, to bear a son. (Her husband was angry because she could not provide him with a male heir.) The queen then promised Cadog that if she did bear a child, she would hand him over to be raised in the service to God (despite, interestingly, the fact that the child – if male – would be the male heir). The miracle happened and Elli eventually took over from Cadog as abbot of the monastery of Llancarfan. Cynics suggest that Elli was Cadog's own son. In any event, St Elli has his own Feast Day (23 January) and two churches named after him, the parish churches of Llanelli (Carmarthenshire) and

Llanelly (Breconshire). The church at Llandybïe was built on the site of a sixth-century memorial to Tybie, the daughter of a Welsh prince called Brychan Brycheiniog, who was killed by natives while preaching Christianity.

The earliest hamlets in Wales included the llan, a public house, and a few cottages. Once these were large enough to be named, llan was almost invariably applied to them (rather than Saint as in England). Here are a few examples from Carmarthenshire:

- **Llangeler** – dedicated to St Celert, a fifth-century saint. St Celert's well is near the church (English name: Celerton).
- **Llangadog** – dedicated to St Cadoc, a fifth-century martyr (Cadocton).
- **Llanfrynach** – dedicated to St Brynach (Bernard).
- **Llansteffan** – founded by Ystyffan, a sixth-century saint and bard. Some derive the name from the dedication of the church to Stephen, the first martyr (Stephen's church).
- **Llanpumpsaint** – dedicated to five brothers (*pump saint*, 'five saints'): Ceitho, Gwyn, Gwynno, Gwynoro and Celynir, who devoted themselves to religious life (Brotherston).
- **Llanddowror** – the village name is a corruption of Llanddyfrgwyr, which meant 'the church of the men of the water'. According to legend, seven sons of Mainaur Mathru were called *Dyfrgwyr* ('water-men'), because they were found in and escaped from the water, and were maintained by fish. They devoted themselves to religious life; hence the church was dedicated to them (Waterton).
- **Llanfihangel-ar-Arth** – dedicated to St Michael, this settlement is situated on a hill above the Teifi. *Ar-arth* or *ar-y-garth* means 'on the hill' (Church Hill).
- **Llanfihangel Abercywyn** – alongside the dual carriageway between Bancyfelin and St Clears is the church of Llanfihangel Abercywyn, built in 1848. It's possible that pilgrims travelling to St Davids may have stopped by to worship at an older church on the site or to take respite from stormy seas. There are six twelfth-century gravestones, showing male and female figures in stylised clothes, carrying weapons and possibly pilgrim staves.

The Christian legacy is not simply confined to place names. For centuries, the Church controlled all aspects of medieval and early modern life in Carmarthenshire – what people ate and drank, their dress and how they entertained themselves. Every community had its visible signs of Church influence. Tithe barns held a tenth of farmers' produce. Ministers delivered sermons at preaching crosses and the remains of one can be seen in the churchyard at St Margaret's church, Pendine. In 1743 Peter Williams, poet and teacher, was inspired by the preaching of George Whitefield at the cross in Lammas Street, Carmarthen. He became known as 'Beibl Peter Williams' and produced scriptural commentaries, which remained popular for generations.

When people sinned, or fell short of what was expected, they faced a range of Church-approved punishments: pillories, stocks, whipping posts, ducking stools and, ultimately, excommunication, which placed them outside the care of the congregation. Other signs of Christianity included mounting steps, once used by parishioners who came to church on horseback. These can still be seen outside Llanegwad and Llandybïe churches. A lych gate, or roofed gateway, was a familiar site outside the entrance to many old churches. The clergyman would traditionally pause at the gate, awaiting the arrival of the coffin bearers. A good example can be seen at Llanelli parish church, opposite Llanelly House, which includes stone seats on either side.

The medieval churches were very different from the relatively cold and bare buildings of today. Rather, they contained bright painted murals and coloured stained-glass windows, gilded carvings, and substantial effigies of knights, their ladies and their children. There are many relics scattered around the county's churches, including ancient chests, mural paintings, pews and galleries. There is a sundial in Llandybïe parish church used to indicate the hours of observance of church services before the days of clocks. There is also an hourglass, set in the pulpit, so that the minister knew the length of his services (spanning at least two hours). As the sermon took on added importance, pews became more popular in churches – they were a luxury before the fifteenth century. In fact, the saying 'having gone to the wall' arises from the time when members of the congregation struggled to stand listening without seats and so retired to the walls for support.

HYWEL DDA GARDEN AND INTERPRETIVE CENTRE

Based in Whitland, the garden and interpretive centre celebrates the achievements of Hywel Dda (Hywel the Good), the tenth-century lawmaker. Hywel Dda created Wales' first formal legal system. He brought together the best minds in Wales to write down laws commonly regarded as very enlightened for the age, especially with regard to women and children. Elsewhere in Europe, women were regarded merely as the property of their menfolk, a status that persisted for centuries. Interestingly under Hywel's Laws, there was no capital punishment for murder. Instead, the murderer's family, extending to the seventh generation, had to pay a murder price to the victim's family. The price varied according to the status of the deceased.

What the Laws Said
- Women could own, buy and sell property.
- Upon a landowner's death, his property had to be divided equally between all his sons – not just those born in wedlock.
- The theft of food was considered acceptable if someone needed food to stay alive.
- Following a murder, the killer and all of his family up to the third or fourth cousin had to pay compensation to the victim's family, up to and including the fourth cousin.
- If a husband was unfaithful, he had to pay his wife a fine of 5s (around three weeks' wages for a craftsman) on the first instance, and £1 the second (about three months' wages).

Hywel had a ruthless side as well, so perhaps he was not as good as he is credited. For example, he ordered the murder of his brother-in-law, Llywarch, in order to take control of Dyfed.

The memorial garden is arranged in sections, each one dedicated to a strand of the law. They relate to:

- Property and contracts.
- How society and families are organised.
- How the king and court operate.
- The rights of women.

In 2013 the National Library of Wales bought a fourteenth-century copy of the laws for £541,250 from the Massachusetts Historical Society of Boston. The medieval manuscript has now been digitised and can be read online by the general public.

THE COMING OF THE NORMANS

The most famous date in English history is 1066. Most schoolchildren are taught that this was when the Saxon hero, Harold, and a French villain, William of Normandy, fought at the Battle of Hastings. In reality, neither had a strong claim to the English throne and both were descendants of the Vikings. The Normans disliked the English, whom they thought were lazy, dirty and drunkards. They set out to replace the language of English with French, cut support for English literature and seized the estates of English landowners. Within twenty years, when William commissioned the extraordinary survey contained within Domesday Book, the Normans owned almost all the land in England. Every pig, cow and yard of land was counted, so much so that an observer likened it to the Day of Judgement. But what did 1066 and all that mean to people in West Wales?

At the time, Wales was made up of several warring kingdoms, including Deheubarth – this covered what we now call Carmarthenshire. Its king, Rhys ap Tewdwr, paid William £40 a year for the right to rule. This ensured good relations with the Normans during his reign. In 1081, William actually passed through the area on his way to the shrine of St David. But when William died in 1087, relations with Deheubarth deteriorated. Rhys was killed in a battle in 1093 seeking to defend his kingdom from Norman invasion.

From the middle of the thirteenth century, Wales became increasingly united under the charismatic leadership of Llewelyn ap Gruffudd, from his stronghold in Gwynedd. One English contemporary said that the Welsh followed Llewelyn 'as if they were glued to him'. Although in 1267 the English monarch acknowledged Llewelyn as Prince of Wales, the first native ruler of Wales to be given the title, the peace between the English and the Welsh did not last.

The last Welsh revolt against the English was led by Owain Glyndŵr (*c*. 1350–1415), considered Wales' second greatest hero (behind Aneurin Bevan) in a poll conducted by Culturenet Cymru in 2003–04. His long-running campaign included capturing the Norman-controlled strongholds of Newcastle Emlyn, Carreg Cennen and Llansteffan, but he lost 700 men when ambushed at Laugharne and St Clears. The English constable at Dinefwr Castle wrote of his anxiety after the Welsh rebel force had burned the town of Carmarthen to the ground, killing fifty men. The constable was convinced that his castle was next to suffer, 'for they have made their vow that they will have us all dead therein'. More than 600 years later,

Owain Glyndŵr

the Glyndŵr Rebellion continues to have symbolic value for many Welsh people. Its destructive force inspired the arson campaign of Meibion Glyndŵr (Sons of Glyndŵr) against English holiday homes during the 1980s. The 'Welsh Braveheart' is still very much alive in the names of streets, restaurants, pubs and monuments throughout the land.

CASTLES

Wales has often been described as a land of castles, with the largest number of castles per square mile in the world. The full story of the medieval castle can be traced in Carmarthenshire, from the earliest simple earth and timber structures (motte and bailey), such as St Clears, to the later big concentric design of Kidwelly Castle. Since the 1960s, the state has increasingly taken over the maintenance of castles from private hands and our knowledge of castle life has improved significantly. We now know that these castles were not only military strongholds. They were homes, courts, administrative centres and social venues for the rich. But, for the Anglo-Normans advancing into Wales, the castle and the knight were their main instruments of power, oppression and status.

Castles were built at strategic, well-defended points to control trade, such as river crossings, and with close access to water. The changing landscape over the centuries makes it sometimes very difficult to picture the earliest castle environments. In Llanelli, for example, Old Castle pond was once the site of an early timber castle – it is now an island in a pond. Across the whole of the county, archaeologists have found forty-three earth castles and the remains of nine built in stone dating to the twelfth and thirteenth centuries. During this period, both the Anglo-Norman and Welsh castle builders and architects were very busy. Carreg Cennen,

The western wiew of Greencastle (Castell Moel) in the County of Carmarthen

A north-east view of Llansteffan Castle

Dryslwyn and Dinefwr were Welsh in origin, while the Normans built Carmarthen, Kidwelly, Llandovery, Laugharne, Llansteffan and Newcastle Emlyn.

Carmarthen

A castle is first mentioned in Carmarthen in 1093, called Rhyd y Gors (Ford of the Marsh). It was timber-built and overlooked the river on the east bank about a mile south of the town. Parts of the present castle date to the early 1100s and it became the Normans' chief administrative centre for south-west Wales. The site of Rhyd y Gors was destroyed when the Great Western Railway was built in the nineteenth century.

Carmarthen Castle has had a chequered history as Welsh and English fought to retain possession. In 1215, Llewelyn the Great captured the castle for the Welsh, only for William Marshal, the 2nd Earl of Pembroke, to regain control for the English in 1223. He may have ordered the building of the major stone walls seen today. Following the attack by Owain Glyndŵr in 1405, the castle needed major repairs. Nearly £100 was spent rebuilding the gatehouse alone, a sum equivalent to around £50,000 today. The gatehouse provided accommodation for the constable who was in charge of the castle. During the seventeenth-century Civil Wars, the Royalists defended the

The southern view of Carmarthen Castle and town

fortification, after which it fell into disrepair. The castle was converted into a prison in the eighteenth and nineteenth centuries, which destroyed the space of the outer ward. It finally became the County Hall.

Carreg Cennen

The castle, situated on a rocky outcrop, is perhaps the most dramatically located in Wales, offering 60-mile panoramic views of the Preseli Hills to the west and the Black Mountain to the south. It was originally built by the Welsh in the twelfth century but taken over by the English. During the Wars of the Roses (1455–85), supporters of the House of Lancaster used the castle as a hideaway. So, in 1462, the opposition army of Yorkist men vandalised the castle with picks and crowbars. The castle is now owned privately although Cadw, Wales' equivalent of English Heritage, looks after the upkeep of the castle.

Dinefwr

Dinefwr has a rich history as the headquarters of the princes of Deheubarth, in South Wales. Gerald of Wales visited the castle in 1188 and records the story of how the castle was nearly lost to the English. In 1163 Prince Rhys ap Gruffudd (Lord Rhys), who owned the castle, was negotiating with Henry II when he was taken prisoner in England. Henry II sent a trusted Breton knight to report on the

Dinefwr Castle from the south

value of the castle and its surroundings. A Welsh guide was instructed to show him the easiest and most pleasant route. Instead, the guide deliberately led him along the hardest terrain, stopping to eat grass, which he claimed was the usual food for locals in times of hardship. When the envoy returned, he declared his disgust that Dinefwr was only fit for wild animals and not worth conquering. Rhys was released from captivity and the castle remained in Welsh hands. It was finally lost to the English during Edward I's Conquest of Wales (1276–84). Following two centuries of control by the English Crown, the castle was leased to Gruffydd ap Nicholas in 1440.

By the thirteenth century, there were two towns nearby. Llandeilo was Welsh and had its own weekly market and annual fair; the other was called 'New towne' and was populated by English families. The gentry built a house named Newton in the fifteenth century and the castle became part of the estate. This was granted to Sir Rhys ap Thomas for his support of Henry VII. When Cadw took over the castle in 1977, it was in a deplorable ruin but substantial repairs were carried out in the 1990s.

Dryslwyn

The castle was first mentioned in 1245 and has an excellent strategic position, built on a steep hill near a major crossing of the River Tywi. When the English besieged the castle in 1287, they used a trebuchet to hurl baskets of river cobbles to kill the Welsh defenders without doing too much harm to the fortifications they hoped to occupy.

Kidwelly

Romantic stories are good for castle tourism, and Kidwelly has the near Welsh equivalent of Robin Hood and Maid Marian. In 1113 a beautiful, intelligent Welsh princess called Gwenllian, the youngest daughter of the King of Gwynedd, fell in love with the visiting Gruffydd ap Rhys, Prince of Deheubarth. The two eloped and set up home in Dinefwr (Llandeilo). At the time, the Anglo-Normans were making inroads into South Wales. The new couple engaged in guerrilla warfare by raiding Norman parties from their woodland and mountain retreats. They seized money and goods from Norman traders and redistributed them among the Welsh poor, or so the legend goes.

In 1136 Gwenllian and her two sons, Morgan and Maelgwm, raised a local army to attack the Normans, while Gruffydd sought reinforcements from Gwynedd. Legend has it that Gwenllian was betrayed by one of her chiefs, who led the Normans to their hideaway in the woods near the castle. The Normans then slaughtered the Welsh in a nearby field to set an example that they should not be crossed. According to the conventions of chivalry, a woman captured should have been shown mercy. Instead, Gwenllian was beheaded (rather than burnt at the stake), the only concession given to her noble pedigree. The bodies of the slain Welshmen were hurled into a deep pit and buried on the battlefield. This became known as *Maes Gwenllian* (Field of Gwenllian), where a miraculous spring apparently welled up on the spot where her decapitated head struck the ground. Her headless ghost is said to roam the area seeking its skull.

The visible remains of Kidwelly Castle today date to the thirteenth and fourteenth centuries. An earlier timber castle had been built in the 1100s but was replaced by stone to provide greater security and permanence. The concentric design, like that at Caerphilly and Beaumaris, reflected the latest military technology; a tall inner curtain wall overlooked a lower outer wall. This enabled archers on both sets of walls to fire at any attacking force simultaneously, effectively doubling the castle's firepower. Before the enemy could reach the interior of the castle, they had to negotiate the drawbridge, with archers firing from the tower, rocks dropped from machicolations above and the heavy outer portcullis. Once through the gate passage, further missiles would have been hurled down from rectangular slots known as murder holes. The castle had a second portcullis and another set of doors at the end of the passage.

The castle was strong enough to act as a storehouse for King Edward I's money when he was travelling to Carmarthen and must have offered sufficient comfort because he stayed for several days in 1283. In about 1390 a major building programme began and included a new gatehouse boasting twenty rooms, including a prison, kitchen, hall and solar, the lord and lady's private room. The word 'solar' here does not refer to sunlight but derives from the French word for 'alone' (*seul*) and conveys the idea of solitary activities, such as reading and embroidery. The castle had become a ruin in the 1600s and was acquired by the Vaughans, the great gentry family. Later it passed to the Cawdors, before the state and then Cadw took over maintenance in the twentieth century.

Edward I

Laugharne

Laugharne Castle was built to control the crossing of the River Taf. The Norman timber castle of the early 1100s was replaced in the thirteenth century by a sturdier one of stone. Burnt buildings and arrowheads point to a Welsh attack led by Llewelyn the Great, who in 1215 overthrew the castles at Laugharne, Llansteffan and

St Clears. The Normans regained the castle and the De Brian family, Lords of Laugharne, carried out major repairs. In 1575 Elizabeth I granted the castle to Sir John Perrot, one of the most colourful characters of the age. He was believed to be one of Henry VIII's illegitimate sons and therefore Elizabeth's stepbrother. He was rich, powerful and argumentative – he once publicly called the queen 'a base bastard'. He was eventually convicted of treason and died in the Tower of London. By that time, Perrot had transformed Laugharne Castle into a Tudor mansion. In 1644, Parliamentarian cannons heavily damaged the castle after a week-long siege. In the late eighteenth century, the Starke family improved appearances by adding a garden. Meanwhile, in more modern times, Dylan Thomas took inspiration writing in the garden summerhouse.

Llandovery

It was a Norman knight called Richard Fitz Pons who is said to have established a castle at Llandovery, overlooking the River Bran, in the early twelfth century. It changed hands many times

Henry IV

and experienced siege after siege, including an attack by Owain Glyndŵr in 1403. A few years before, King Henry IV visited the castle. The end was nigh when the Welsh destroyed the castle in 1532 – locals helped themselves to stones for their own buildings. Mrs Sinclair, a tourist, visited the ruin in 1839 and described it as 'an old Stilton cheese making its last appearance on the table'.

Llansteffan

A double ditch on the western side of the present site is a reminder that a sixth-century Iron Age hill fort once stood here. The Normans built an earth and timber castle in between these prehistoric remains. The beach below was used to bring in supplies. Control of the castle switched between the Normans and the Welsh during the twelfth century, before it was converted into a wealthy fifteenth-century home.

Newcastle Emlyn

Newcastle Emlyn

The unusual thing about Newcastle Emlyn is that it has the region's only stone castle built by the native Welsh. Although the Normans erected a fort in the 1100s, the Welsh prince, Maredudd ap Rhys, built the new castle by 1240. The accounts tell us that at the height of the building work, in 1226, carpenters were paid 9*d* a day – 100 years later, their wages had fallen to 3*d* a day. Men, women, boys and girls were all employed at various times in building projects.

The castle was subjected to the usual Welsh/Norman skirmishes. King Edward I, nicknamed 'Longshanks' because of his height, visited as part of his campaign to subdue the Welsh. The castle remained under the king's control, although it suffered under the Glyndŵr rebellion of 1403. Sir Rhys ap Thomas, friend of Henry VII, restored the castle as a secondary home (to Carew Castle) in the 1500s. It then became more of a home than a military stronghold, although it was battered again during the Civil Wars.

A full-length view of Edward I, showing his great height

Aside from castle building, the Normans transformed Carmarthenshire in other ways. They turned the old Roman town of Carmarthen into an international trade centre. It evolved from a remote military outpost to the most advanced town in Wales. Ships sailed up the estuary to the first crossing point on the river to unload barrels of French wine and food. In the 1390s, John Owen was the leading wool trader and his business was worth £450 a year (around £220,000 today). To illustrate the prosperity of the area, the household of the wonderfully named Llywelyn ap Gruffydd Fychan of Caeo, among the wealthiest of the Carmarthenshire gentry, was said to have consumed the equivalent of fifty-five bottles of wine a day! In 1332, Carmarthen was made the only staple port in Wales. Medieval staple rights meant that merchant ships had to unload their goods at the port, and then display them for sale for a short period, usually a few days. Only after the local customers had had the opportunity to buy could the merchants reload their ships and travel onwards to sell their remaining stock. Carmarthen had the rights to sell to foreigners five commodities: wool, pelts, leather, lead and tin.

PLAGUE AND WARS

Carmarthenshire's late medieval economy was fragile and suffered from the demands from London for higher taxes, and the vagaries of poor harvests, wars and plagues. As if that wasn't enough, the region was hit by plague at various times in the medieval period. In the sixth century, bubonic plague was brought into Wales by flea-infested rats on board trading ships from the South of France. St Teilo's biographer described it as coming over the land like the 'column of a watery cloud'. With unburied bodies lying around, the circumstances were rife for the so-called Yellow Plague (cholera) to add misery to the decimated population. In the early 1900s, nearly 500 male skeletons were reportedly discovered at Llangendeirne when the church was being restored. They were laid without any covering and piled on top of each other. It is possible that these were the remains of monks who were victims of the plague, buried on a former monastic site.

During the fourteenth century, Europe was overwhelmed by the Black Death, which claimed around 25 million victims between

1348 and 1350 alone. About one in four lost their lives in Wales, the majority of victims in 1349. These included the two harbour officials at Carmarthen quayside who, on the front line as it were, inevitably fell victim. The plague spread quickly through the nearby village of Llanllwch. Fairs were cancelled, taverns emptied and there were fewer people to govern the towns. Death came within days. Once purple blotches – or 'buboes' – appeared on the body, survival chances were slim.

Wars also took their toll on the people of Carmarthenshire. Field names tell us something about the bloodshed of the Middle Ages. For example, around Aberglasney the fields still have names that commemorate a battle of 1272, such as Cae Tranc (field of vengeance) and Cae'r Ochain (groaning field). The area supplied 1,200 archers at the battle of Crécy in 1346 and a further 240 at the Battle of Agincourt in 1415, playing a key role in Henry V's victory. The men were recruited or mustered at Carmarthen. We know the names of some individuals who took up arms, such as Philip Bennett of St Clears, Thomas Cooke and Philip ap Adda of Laugharne, and Richard ap Gruffydd of Caeo. The men were paid for 45.5 days from the revenues of John Merbury, the chamberlain of South Wales. All these troops probably took the same road from Carmarthen, across South Wales to Brecon and then to Hereford and south to Southampton. When they passed through Warminster (Wiltshire), the townspeople complained that Welsh (and English) soldiers had taken food without payment. Around 400 actually fought at Agincourt (out of a total force of 8,000) but there are no records of any casualties. They were highly skilled men, firing fifteen arrows a minute over 150yds. Shakespeare, writing in the 1590s, did much to present the Welsh archers in a good light and refers to the adoption of the leek, which became the national emblem:

> Your majesty says very true: if your majestie is remembered of it, the Welshmen did good service in a garden where leeks did grow, wearing leeks in their Monmouth caps; which, your majesty knows, to this hour is an honourable badge of the service; and I do believe your majesty takes no scorn to wear the leek upon Saint Davy's day.
>
> Fluellen, *Henry V*, Act IV, Scene 7

In fact, the vast majority of archers at Agincourt were English rather than Welsh.

TUDOR CARMARTHENSHIRE

Life in Carmarthenshire during the sixteenth and seventeenth centuries was full of contradictions. It was an age when almost everyone believed in God. Not believing in God was like not believing in rivers, trees or mountains. The logic was simple: creation required a creator, just as houses had builders. Atheism did not appear as a word until the 1580s. Everyone was expected to attend church to hear sermons and observe rituals. Everyone was expected to pray when getting up in the morning, before meals, during the evening and at bedtime. Everyone was expected to observe holy days and the rules of the Church on how to lead a godly life. Yet it was also an age of superstition, magic and pagan beliefs. This was particularly so in the countryside. Everyone believed that they were at the mercy of supernatural powers, which could be calmed through spells and magic.

The Tudor age is often seen as one of relative peace, security, law and order, following the bloody Wars of the Roses. This was the impression created by loyal Tudor supporters, including William Shakespeare, keen to distance their time from the bloodshed and anarchy ending with the reign of Richard III. When Henry Tudor defeated Richard at the battle of Bosworth in 1485 he did so thanks to the efforts of Rhys ap Thomas, prominent gentleman and Mayor of Carmarthen, whose tomb can be seen in St Peter's church. It was Rhys who placed the crown upon the new king's head following his victory over Richard III at Bosworth Field. But Thomas' allegiance was not a foregone conclusion. He had previously declared the following oath to Richard:

Richard III

> Whoever ill-affected to the state, shall dare to land in those parts of Wales where I have any employment under your majesty, must resolve with himself to make his entrance and irruption over my belly.

The legend has it that after Henry Tudor's return to Britain (at Dale, Pembrokeshire, in 1485) Rhys eased his conscience by hiding under Mullock Bridge, Dale, as Henry marched over, thus absolving himself of his oath to Richard.

Henry VII's reforms were generally welcomed by leading Welsh figures. When Wales was brought into union with England under the Acts of Union, this meant that all were (in theory) subject to the same laws. It is widely accepted that Wales did experience greater stability as a result of the Acts of Union. But it was still an age of brutality; pain and cruelty were part of everyday life. Burning at the stake, cutting off hands and ears, public whippings and humiliation in the pillory, stocks or ducking stool were all common practices. The spire of Abergwili church is said to include part of the stone cross, reputed to have held Bishop Ferrar when he was martyred in Carmarthen market place on 30 March 1555 for refusing to recant his Protestant faith. The former Poet Laureate Ted Hughes, a descendant of Ferrar on his mother's side, describes the martyrdom as Ferrar refused to flinch at the stake:

> Out of his mouth, fire like a glory broke,
> And smoke burned his sermon into the skies

In 1902 a memorial plaque was placed at the site of the old market place in Nott Square (inside the railings of Nott's Monument). It reads:

> The noble army of Martyrs praise thee.
> Near this spot suffered for the truth
> Saturday, March 30th, 1555
> Dr Robert Ferrar, Bishop of St David's.
> We shall by God's grace light such a candle
> In England, as shall never be put out.
>
> Erected by a Protestant of this town.

The Protestant Reformation changed the appearance of Carmarthenshire's churches. It brought to an end profits from the sale of candles and masses, removed images and frescoes from churches, ended the trade in miraculous relics, and replaced altars with communion tables. An untold amount of damage was done to church buildings as they were stripped of their ornaments and simplified for worship. Protestant reformers wanted to sweep away doctrine such as purgatory and practices of buying 'indulgences'. They believed that faith alone was necessary for salvation.

The wealthy were quick to take advantage of the opportunities afforded by the sale of the monasteries and religious houses in the 1530s. In Carmarthen, the priory was sold but not demolished until the nineteenth century, when it was cleared to make way for a tinworks. Carmarthen Friary became the town's first grammar school in 1543. Elsewhere, the monastic houses at Talley, Whitland and Kidwelly Priory were stripped of their lead, plate and glass, to be sold off to raise money for the Crown. Religious houses which had an income of more than £200 were allowed to continue. Unfortunately, Talley Abbey was valued at £136 and was forced to close.

The new wealth was kept within the hands of a minority – the gentry, large-scale farmers and merchants – no more than

20 per cent of the county's population. The other 80 per cent, made up of tenant farmers, labourers and the very poor, had to contend with higher rents and the price of ordinary goods increasing fourfold between 1530 and 1640. Although food production increased, it could not keep pace with the expansion in population and so prices rose. Those at the bottom of society suffered most: widows, orphans, wounded soldiers, the disabled, mentally ill, tramps, starving youths, Egyptians (gypsies) and the elderly.

It was difficult not to notice 'the poor' in Tudor Carmarthenshire. The market town of Carmarthen in particular attracted many Irish beggars, as it was on the main overland route from Ireland to London. Scraps of food were more likely to be obtained at the busy Carmarthen port. But every town and village had those who had fallen on hard times. By the end of the sixteenth century, the authorities considered that the number of 'vagabonds and idel' had become intolerable, forcing the introducing of new legislation known as the Poor Laws. In 1597 overseers were appointed in every parish, responsible for ensuring that all children who could not be cared for by their parents were placed as apprentices at the parishioners' expense. The responsibility for the poor was no longer a matter left to charity and the churches. Rather, poor relief or support became a secular responsibility and has remained so ever since. The Tudors also tried to distinguish between those who should work and those who could not. The government had already introduced some stern measures to deal with the 'undeserved'. In 1563 all villagers and townspeople were forced to pay towards the upkeep of the local poor or be fined. In 1572, an Act was passed declaring that those roaming around towns (vagabonds) over the age of 14 were to be 'whipped and burned through the gristle of the right ear with a hot iron unless some credible person will take him into service for a year'.

The depiction of the Tudor period as a 'golden era' was strengthened through the reign of Elizabeth I (1558–1603). It was certainly an age for exploring new lands and ideas, new advances in science and technology, such as printing, and major works of literature, including Bishop Morgan's Welsh Bible of 1588. By the

Elizabeth I

start of Elizabeth's reign, Carmarthen was the largest town in Wales but still very small by modern-day standards. In 1566 it had 328 households compared to 200 in Tenby, 101 in Kidwelly and twelve in Llanelli. The overall population of Carmarthen was around 2,000, double the size of Cardiff. Kidwelly, which had been the main rival to Carmarthen throughout the medieval period, declined in status because the River Gwendraeth silted up, making it difficult for ships to dock. Laugharne, meanwhile, enjoyed greater prosperity under the control of Sir John Perrott, who was one of the most powerful figures in Tudor Wales.

The top echelons of Carmarthenshire society had no qualms about taking legal action against each other. Records from the Star Chamber, the leading Elizabethan court at Westminster, include the case of John Thomas, a gentleman from Llangadog, who claimed that Sir John Vaughan of Golden Grove and his servant got him so drunk that he signed away his hereditary lands. In another case, William Parry, the Sheriff of Carmarthen and Justice of the Peace, took action against another JP for urging a crowd to assault him at a church service after he refused to support the marriage of his 14-year-old daughter. Unfortunately we do not know the outcomes of these cases.

A sense of everyday life in Elizabethan Carmarthen can be gleaned from surviving town records. Fines were given out for a wide range of offences, including allowing pigs to wander the streets and opening taverns during church service. There were frequent complaints about corrupt market traders and those found guilty were fined heavily. The Carmarthen market was held on three days during the week, Wednesday, Friday and Saturday, and attracted hordes of people from the countryside. The town streets were packed with animals to be sold, alongside merchants, travellers, families, vagabonds, and thieves. A tax of between 2d and 4d had to be paid on every animal sold at market, while merchants were required to pay an annual tax of £5 per annum.

Pirates and smugglers were a nuisance to the shipping that frequented the busy Bristol Channel. In 1592, Carmarthen merchants complained to the Privy Council in London about pirates who had robbed them of 'silks, wine and oil to the value of £10,000' (equivalent to more than £1.2 million today). On the other hand, some well-respected dealers were not averse to buying illicit goods.

Getting around Elizabethan Carmarthenshire posed its problems. In fact, the word 'road' did not appear until the 1560s. The highways and tracks were in a very poor state and remained so until the late eighteenth century, as ordinary people travelled by foot or horseback. The Continental fashion of using coaches started to appeal to the well-to-do travellers in Tudor Wales. However, very few roads were paved and most were in a deplorable condition, especially during winter months. Their upkeep was the responsibility of each community but those who were expected to carry out repairs hardly used the roads. The distance covered in a day depended on many factors, such as the driver's equestrian skills, the road condition, the weather and the horse's physical condition. Horses needed stops to replace shoes, to feed, drink and rest. It might have taken up to a week to ride more than 200 miles from Carmarthen to London. In 1524, Sir Edward Don left his residence in Buckinghamshire to visit his ancestral home in Kidwelly. He kept a daily record of his journey, noting his spending on matters such as saddles, clothes, bed and breakfast, ale, gifts and servants. He tells us that on a visit to Carmarthen he bought a looking glass, some Portuguese clothes, apples, mustard and candles.

Many of Carmarthenshire's highways followed the medieval and Roman routes. But these were not suitable for waggons and coaches. Even single horse riders struggled; in 1652 a traveller described being stuck with his horse in a quagmire on his way back from Cardiganshire. By the early 1800s, the Milford mail coach could only travel at a speed of 3–4mph because of the bumpy state of the roads. It would take several days to get from London to Carmarthen – in 1794, two waggons left London each Saturday and arrived in Carmarthen on the following Tuesday. Visitors to 'the miserable village of Llanelly' were influenced by the poor state of the road approaching from the village of Llannon. They struggled with water-filled potholes in the winter and clouds of dust in the summer.

CARMARTHENSHIRE IN THE SEVENTEENTH AND EIGHTEENTH CENTURIES

One of the things that would strike a modern-day visitor transported back to Carmarthenshire 300 or so years ago would be the scarcity of people. The population of the county was no more than 35,000 – around a sixth of present-day numbers. It has been estimated that the population density was roughly one person to every 14 acres compared with one person to every 3 acres today. Carmarthen had around 1,000 people; Kidwelly and Llanelli something like 500 each; Llansteffan no more than 250 and Ammanford did not exist. Many people lived in scattered farms and hamlets. John Speed's map of Carmarthen in 1610 shows the rural nature of the town with open fields and spaces and few roads.

The homes of seventeenth-century Carmarthenshire people varied just as they do today. The very rich lived in great mansions set in beautiful parks such as Dinefwr, most of the 'middling sort' owned or rented detached houses, and the poor rented rooms in townhouses or were rural tenants in farmhouses. The very poor did not have a home and lived on the streets, under the hedges or in the woods. Large windows were expensive and beyond the means of most people, whose houses had wooden shutters rather than glazed panels. Candles and rush lights provided artificial lighting for most homes. Candles were made up of a wick, usually of flax or cotton, thickly coated with wax or tallow (fat). Local newspapers, such as the *Carmarthen Journal*, carried adverts for tallow candles through to the early twentieth century and they remained an important source of domestic lighting, particularly in rural areas of the county.

What did everyday life mean for the different social ranks?

The Poor
Today there are plenty of sources to tell us about people's experiences of poverty – films, documentaries, personal testimonies, newspaper reports, books and magazines, chat shows, reports by social welfare services, charities and religious organisations. A recent report by the Joseph Rowntree Foundation found that

almost 700,000 people in Wales live in poverty – nearly a quarter of the population. In relative terms, this means that they fall below the average family income and do not have enough money to meet their basic needs. In West Wales, including Carmarthenshire, rural poverty remains a big problem – one in five children in the county are raised in poverty.

However, we cannot retrace poor people's thinking in the distant past, as they could not read or write to record their thoughts. Historians like David Howell have done their best to piece together something of the lives of the poor, by making the most of parish registers, gaol files, and snippets from court proceedings and estate records. Unfortunately, the poor often appear in history when they experience some form of suffering or have done something wrong. We know that many people lived on the edge, surviving on a day-by-day basis, because of their inadequate incomes, uncertain harvests, killer diseases, growing family sizes and strained relationships with landlords.

It is worth clarifying who made up 'the poor', because it is such a very broad term. Some of the poor were tenant farmers who leased their smallholding (a farmhouse and a few acres) from a landowner. Others were the masses of labourers who worked the farms, ports and streets. These included men, women and children hoeing, weeding and picking stones from the fields. Few farm servants were paid wages for working the land. Rather, they were provided with accommodation, sleeping in an outbuilding – usually the loft over a barn. At the lowest end of the social ladder were the homeless, vagabonds and tramps.

The scale of poverty in the sixteenth and seventeenth centuries should not be underestimated. In Carmarthenshire, we know that in 1670 around one in five people were paupers – without any means of support. This is based on the fact that they were unable to pay what was called The Hearth Tax (or chimney money), introduced by Parliament in 1662, to support the lifestyle of the monarchy. For each hearth or fireplace, a shilling was payable every six months. In contrast to the poor, the Vaughans of Llanelly House had twelve hearths in 1670.

The hearth had symbolic importance for families in Wales. The great folk historian Iorwerth Peate, in his classic book *The Welsh House*, said that the hearth was 'the place of honour near the fire, where the guests are invited to sit down'. The stone that was placed vertically behind the fire was called the *pentanfaen* (fireback stone) and in medieval times it was an offence to remove it, even if the house had been destroyed. There were nineteenth-century reports that in Welsh farmhouses the fire had been kept alight every night year after year, some for centuries.

According to Welsh custom, a man and his family could settle on wasteland if they erected a building between sunset and sunrise, and had a fire in the hearth by morning. The surrounding land, at a radius of the throw of an axe, also became their property. During the late eighteenth and early nineteenth centuries, many people succeeded in building these *tai unnos* (one-night houses) in the allotted time frame. People were forced to take such action because so much land was being enclosed as farmers moved over to sheep farming. These houses have long since disappeared. However, many isolated cottages dotted around Carmarthenshire were built on the site of these former one-night houses.

One night in September 2006 Dorian Bowen, a chartered surveyor from Trelech a'r Betws, decided to have a go at building a *tŷ unnos* on his land. Sixty of his family and friends (dressed in period costume) worked through a stormy night gathering local materials – gorse and straw for the thatched roof, oak for the roof supports, turf for the walls and hazel for the wickerwork chimney. The process of building the house created a spirit and energy (*hwyl*), reaffirming family and community bonds. Aside from the under-floor heating and contemporary bathroom, the interior design and furniture is in keeping with life in the 1700s and the house is now a holiday rental home offering the most authentic interior cottage in Wales. It is also possible to see an original Carmarthenshire cottage built of clay, known locally as *clom*, which has been re-erected at the National Museum of Wales (St Fagans). The simply furnished Nant Wallter cottage was built in 1770 for farm labourers on the Taliaris estate, near Llandeilo.

In their everyday lives, the people of Carmarthenshire faced the very real persistent danger of fire, floods and harvest failures. After burglary, fire was the most serious threat to people's homes. A spark could easily ignite a thatched roof and fires spread quickly among timber-framed properties in narrow streets. In 1633 Thomas Atkins, the Mayor of Carmarthen, ordered the purchase of 'twelve buckets with two hooks to pull the burning thatch off the roofs, and iron hats for the firemen'. This was the first reference to a fire service in the county.

Craftsmen and Traders

Trades in towns such as Carmarthen were organised into guilds or associations. There were guilds for all sorts of trades, including tanners, weavers, shoemakers, hatters and ironsmiths. Here is a list of traders present in Carmarthen during the sixteenth and seventeenth centuries:

Cordwainers	made fine, soft leather shoes
Cutlers	made cutlery
Feltmakers	made felt
Fullers	fulled (cleaned and thickened) cloth
Glovers	made and sold gloves
Goldsmiths	metalworkers, specialists in gold
Hatters	made and sold hats
Ironsmiths	blacksmiths who made objects from wrought iron or steel
Pewterers	made pewter utensils or containers
Plumbers	fitted and repaired water pipes
Shearmen	sheared cloth
Shoemakers	made shoes and other footwear
Silversmiths	made silver articles
Tanners	tanned animal hides
Tinkers	travelled around mending pans and other utensils
Tailors	fitted clothes
Weavers	weaved fabric

A new beaver and felt hat industry emerged in Carmarthen around 1633 when the enterprising Lewis Lloyd, a hatter, petitioned to be a burgess of the town. The council decided that as there were no such tradesmen in the town he should be allowed to begin trading, provided he paid a certain fee and agreed not to 'meddle with any trade or exercise any other mystery, but only the trade of a hatter'. To join a guild, craftsmen served a seven-year apprenticeship and were required to follow strict rules. Hostility existed between those who plied their trade outside the guild in country cottages and paid-up members in the towns.

From time to time, trade was badly affected by crop failures and plague. Carmarthen suffered five major outbreaks of plague, in 1604, 1606, 1611, 1651 and 1657. In 1653 on the Felinfoel road at Llanelli, men were posted to keep watch and prevent strangers from entering the town. Traders were expected to leave their goods in the place known as Cae Watch (Capel Newydd), or Cae'r Halen, and money passed through a stone vessel filled with salt-water, which served as a disinfectant. There were many different views of the cause, the most popular being that it was due to 'miasma' or bad air, polluted by filth, overcrowding, dunghills, excrement and stinking standing water. In some great towns and cities such as London, cats, dogs and pigeons were killed. Yet Kidwelly's coat of arms and official seal, which adorn the signs entering the town, shows a black cat. Legend has it that this was the first animal seen alive after the plague hit the town. It received the honour of being a symbol of deliverance. There was no known cure but a host of preventive measures were used, including chewing tobacco, wearing herb-filled pomanders around the neck, fasting and prayer.

Gentry

There were a few well-to-do families who ruled Carmarthenshire. They were the Members of Parliament, Justices of the Peace, employers, high sheriffs and patrons of the Church. All key decisions were made through them. From the cradle to the grave, life for the gentry was very different from others in society. Their sons and daughters were educated by private tutors or at public schools and then universities, although the children of the lesser gentry attended cathedral or grammar schools such as St David's or Carmarthen. The very rich travelled around the Continent, following a grand tour of countries such as Italy, France and

Switzerland from where they returned with books, maps, antiques and works of art. Of course, the gentry from England and elsewhere also toured Wales as tourists.

In 1684 Henry Somerset, the first Duke of Beaufort and Lord President of the Council in Wales, visited each of the Welsh counties so that he could examine the state of the army and meet local magistrates and the gentry. It was a spectacular piece of theatre. He was attended by hundreds of uniformed officers and servants. Among the travelling party was Thomas Dineley, who kept a diary of the journey. In it he describes the reception at Carmarthen where there was a ringing of bells, shouting, free-flowing wine for the general public and bonfires.

The gentry enjoyed lavish garden parties, listened to music, put on amateur dramatics and played cards, cricket and billiards. Their favourite 'sports' were otter hunting and fishing in the summer, and fox hunting and shooting in the winter. Golden Grove, the Vaughan estate, kept its own private packs of beagles and huntsmen. The 'great folk' often spent their winters in London.

It is easy to get the impression that there was never a dull moment for the gentry. In fact, much of their everyday life was monotonous and revolved around ceremonies and duties. For the lesser gentry, particularly those living out of town, there were very few highlights. In the 1780s Jane Johnes, the daughter of a squire at Dolaucothi, kept a diary. She records how she spent her time as an 18-year-old, minding the chickens, attending to the garden and in needlework. Occasionally she had the joy of visiting one of the greater gentry houses.

It was the Christian duty of gentlemen and ladies to help the poor and many chose to leave money in their wills. In 1644, the vicar of Llandovery, Rees Prichard, left 150 acres of oak woodland to be cut for the poor to use as fuel when required. Atwell Taylor (d. 1640), who was a Carmarthen merchant, bequeathed 'to the poor of Carmarthen 20 shillings to be distributed according to the customs of the same place'.

The wealthiest Carmarthenshire families were the Vaughans of Golden Grove and the Rices of Newton, multimillionaires of their day.

MAJOR CARMARTHENSHIRE GENTRY HOMES

The Vaughans (Cawdors) of Golden Grove (Gelli Aur), Llanfihangel Aberbythych
The Vaughans of Golden Grove were very well connected, mixing in the royal circles of King James I and Charles I. John Vaughan (1640–1713) pursued his scientific interests in London as president of the Royal Society. The famous diarist Samuel Pepys, who recorded the Great Fire of London, described Vaughan as 'one of the lewdest fellows of the age', a somewhat hypocritical statement, given Pepys' own multiple sexual encounters with servants and girls who worked in shops, taverns and on the street.

Oliver Cromwell

When the last of the Vaughan family, John Vaughan (1757–1804), died without any male heirs, he left his 28,000-acre Golden Grove estate to his friend John Campbell, the then Lord Cawdor. The Cawdors also acquired properties in Llanelli and Carmarthen, lead mines at Rhandirmwyn and several collieries in the Gwendraeth Valley and Llanelli. The Cawdors were Scottish, based at Cawdor Castle in Nairn, near Inverness. Their most famous ancestor was Macbeth (popularised in Shakespeare's play and the line, 'All hail Macbeth! Hail to thee, Thane of Cawdor!'). By 1883, the Cawdors owned 100,000 acres, including 34,000 acres in Carmarthenshire. Their annual income from rents was £45,000 (equivalent to more than £2 million today). The family was among the top thirty landowners in the UK.

The present-day Golden Grove mansion was built in 1826 and is the third house to be built on the site. During the Second World War, the American Air Force used the mansion and in 1952 it was leased to the council as an agricultural college. In recent times, a rare and frank insight into the Cawdor family has been provided in a memoir, *Title Deeds*, by Lady Elizabeth Campbell. She recalls how her father, Hugh John Vaughan Campbell (1932–93), squandered the family's wealth through a life ruined by domestic violence, drugs, drink and extramarital affairs.

The Rices (Dynevors) of Newton House, Llandeilo

Newton House is set within the historically rich Dinefwr Park. The grounds include the remains of two Roman forts (one of which is second in size only to the legionary fortress at Caerleon), a medieval castle, eighteenth-century landscaped gardens and a Victorian church. There was a house here in the fifteenth century associated with the Rhys (Rice) family but it was replaced in 1660 (the date on one of the roof timbers). Between 1760 and 1780, the house was romanticised by the addition of turrets and battlements, while Capability Brown, the leading landscape gardener of the age, had a hand in the design of the grounds. In the 1850s the house was further remodelled in a Gothic design, with the present tower added. By the 1970s the house had fallen into disrepair and was sold by Lord Dynevor. Many of the original features had been stripped away and beams removed for firewood. In the 1980s and '90s, the National Trust acquired the deer park, grounds and house, and restoration work has included a project to present rooms in the style of 1912. The exhibition on the first floor tells the story of the history and landscape of Dinefwr. The park includes fallow deer and a small herd of Dinefwr White Park Cattle.

Since the First World War, many of the gentry's houses in Carmarthenshire have gradually fallen into ruin. Many sons of heritage properties served and died in both world wars. Understandably, their grieving parents did not have the will or the finances to keep their houses going when they faced the loss of succession, high taxes, and major social and political changes.

One depressing example is the story of Edwinsford (Llansawel). Once a superior eighteenth-century home, by the 1940s it had become derelict after nineteen generations as the Williams family home. Polish refugees were reported to be growing mushrooms under the floorboards during the Second World War, which only added to the rot.

RELIGION, POLITICS AND THE CIVIL WARS

In the 1640s, Parliament's struggle with King Charles I over the manner of governing England and Wales, religious policies and the role of the monarch, resulted in the Civil Wars (1642–48). The conflict was not greeted with much enthusiasm in Carmarthenshire, although the county's leading gentry were generally supportive of the King, as was most of Wales. Oliver Cromwell and his Parliamentarians drew support from south Pembrokeshire, as Tenby and Pembroke relied on a flourishing sea trade with Bristol, which was controlled by Cromwell's forces.

Although the Royalists built huge earthworks to defend Carmarthen town, they surrendered to the Parliamentarian troops after only a week's resistance in 1644. These defensive ditches and banks were called the Bulwarks and the remains can still be seen opposite the Tesco superstore along Water Street. They are the best examples of surviving Royalist town defences in Britain. At the end of the war, three captured Royalist leaders, Rowland Laugharne, Jon Poyer and Rice Powell, were sent to London. In April 1649, they were court-martialled and executed by firing squad. Strangely, it was decided that the sentence would be carried out on only one of them, determined by lots – Colonel Poyer was the unfortunate one chosen and was executed at Covent Garden on 25 April.

In 1648 Cromwell himself visited Carmarthen and asked for weapons and food to be provided for his army it was about to besiege Pembroke Castle, which had been taken up by the King's supporters. Cromwell stayed in Carmarthen again in 1649 en route to Ireland. Cromwell and his Puritans have not had a good press – the term 'puritanical' became a term of abuse, although originally it referred to followers who had a pure soul. Puritans were deeply concerned about what they considered to be a decline in moral standards. Fines were issued for swearing, games banned on Sundays and the excesses of Christmas outlawed.

There were nineteen Puritan ministers in Carmarthenshire, of whom Stephen Hughes (1622–88) was the most influential. He ministered at Meidrim and would ride up to 10 miles between his sermons, which he preached twice a week. He wanted ordinary people to get closer to God by reading the Bible and so he supported the work of a body known as the Welsh Trust (1674–81), which opened schools to teach poor children how to read, write and count. He also published a number of religious books in Welsh and fulfilled his dream of producing a cheap Bible in Welsh. In 1688 he also translated John Bunyan's most famous work, *The Pilgrim's Progress*, into Welsh.

Critics of a new movement known as 'Baptists' first used the term in the seventeenth century – although it wasn't until the nineteenth century that Baptists accepted the name themselves. Baptists were persecuted because they held Christ, rather than the monarch, as head of the church. By the 1650s we know that groups of Baptists were meeting in Carmarthen and Llanelli. The Llanelli Baptists crossed the River Loughor to join services at Ilston church on the Gower, where the congregation grew from 50 to 250 by 1660. Their minister John Myles received a salary of £40 from Oliver Cromwell's government to serve as public preacher in the region. He left for America when the monarchy was restored in 1660.

George Fox formed the Quakers during the 1650s. One story suggests that the name comes from when Fox told a magistrate to tremble (quake) at the name of God. Officially, they are called the Society of Friends or the Religious Society of Friends. By the mid-eighteenth century, a Quaker meeting house had been established in Lammas Street (Carmarthen), known as Quakers' Yard, and also in Llandovery.

George Fox (Library of Congress, LC-USZ62-5790)

The first Jews are thought to have settled in Wales during the thirteenth century when the English built castles and walled towns. Edward I may have expelled them because he could not repay their loans, which paid for his expensive programme of castle-building in Wales.

Very little is known about the history of the Jews in West Wales before the twentieth century. Jewish shopkeepers were attacked during the Tredegar riots of 1911 but the Jews had resided in towns such as Llanelli since the 1800s without any reported tensions. A synagogue was opened in Swansea in 1859 and another built in Llanelli in 1909, at the junction of Erw Road and Queen Victoria Road. Conservative politician Michael Howard is the son of a synagogue cantor (an official responsible for music) who moved from Transylvania to Llanelli in the 1930s.

In the fifty or so years between 1780 and 1830, everyday life in Carmarthenshire was transformed. People had to adjust to the major changes brought by the Agricultural and Industrial Revolutions. For centuries, those who worked small farms did enough to get by and feed the family, ever mindful of the need to pay the rent. Any surplus was sold at the local markets, but this marginal existence was only sustainable if conditions remained stable. However, the increase in the population, as a result of a higher birth rate and reduced death rate, meant that there were more mouths to feed. Within two generations, the population of Wales doubled from 530,000 (1780) to over a million (1850).

This is despite the fact that the infant mortality rate remained very high by modern standards. Diseases such as smallpox claimed many young lives or left survivors horribly scarred. In 1722–23, seventy-one people died of the disease in Carmarthen, and further severe outbreaks followed over the next few years. Although life hung in the balance for many young people, the average Welshman or woman was healthier than people in most other countries. In 1740, life expectancy in Britain was thirty-seven years compared with twenty-eight in France. For every 1,000 births in Britain, 190 babies died; in France it was more like 280, and it was even worse in Spain and Russia.

A flavour of economic life in Carmarthen town towards the end of the eighteenth century can be seen in a listing of trades for 1794:

- Baylis and Lewis – Mercers (cloth sellers)
- Bowen, David – Mercer
- Campbell, John – Lead Smelter and Proprietor of the Mines
- Charles, Mr – Roper
- Daniel, John – Printer, Bookseller and Stationer
- Davis, Mr – Mercer

- Evans, Griffith – Hardware man
- Griffiths, John – Hatter and Hosier
- Humphreys, John – Innkeeper (Ivy Bush)
- James, Mr – Brazier (worked with brass)
- Lewis, David – Tanner
- Lewis, David – Roper
- Lewis, Henry – Merchant
- Lewis, Morgan – Merchant
- Lewis, Sarah – Ironmonger
- Lewis, Thomas – Grocer
- Llewellin, Josiah – Merchant and Tallow Chandler
- Morgan, John – Mercer
- Morgan, Philip – Shipbuilder
- Morgan, William – Timber Merchant
- Morley, David – Cabinet Maker
- Morris and Hughes – Merchants
- Morris, William – Merchant
- Owen, Jeremiah – Maltster (brewer, maker or seller of malts)
- Phillips, Mrs – Tanner
- Rees, John – Merchant
- Ross, John – Printer, Bookseller and Stationer
- Rowe, Miss – Maltster
- Scott, Walter – Nursery and Seedman
- Stonehewer, Hugh – Innkeeper (Boar's Head)
- Stacey, Mr – Mercer
- Taylor, Thomas – Mercer and Wine Merchant
- Thomas, Miss – Mercer
- Thomas, Samuel and Co. – Ropers
- Timmers, Joseph – Hardware man
- Vaughan, Philip – Ironfounder
- Webb, Mr – Mercer and Tea Dealer
- Williams, Martha and Co. – Ironmongers
- Williams, John – Ironmonger
- Williams, John – Brazier
- Williams, William – Brazier

The expanding international trade routes meant that for those who could afford it, shops offered a wide range of goods. The people of Laugharne, for example, could buy white and brown sugar, soap, spices, fruit, tobacco, cups, door-locks, frying pans, buttons, coloured cloth and all kinds of household tools. The 1794 list is by no means exhaustive however, and does not reflect fully the vibrancy of economic life in eighteenth-century Carmarthen. For example, John Ross was one of many involved in the town's printing and book trade, which made Carmarthen the leading centre in Wales. Ross Avenue in the town is named after him. Books in English and Welsh flowed out from the presses in Lanmaes Street, King Street, Priory Street and Spilman Street. But it was said of John Ross that he printed nearly as many books as all the other printers in Wales together.

The *Carmarthen Journal* was launched on 3 March 1810 and remains the oldest surviving newspaper in Wales. The thirst for knowledge led to further newspapers being circulated, notably the *Welshman* in 1832, which continued through to the Second World War.

VICTORIAN AND EDWARDIAN CARMARTHENSHIRE (1837–1910)

The sixty-four years of Queen Victoria's reign (1837–1901) has been described in glowing terms as the age of improvement. There is no doubt that there was much progress in Victorian Carmarthenshire, like other parts of Wales. Anyone who lived through Victoria's reign witnessed remarkable change: the way people travelled, communicated, ate, dressed, shopped and dealt with sickness was transformed. For the first time in history, the people of Carmarthenshire could travel by train, attend school for free, see themselves and their loved ones preserved in a photograph, ride a bicycle, eat ice cream and tinned foods, send a telegraph, borrow books from a public library, play rugby, read cheap magazines and newspapers, and, at least for men, vote (women over the age of 30 and with certain property were first able to vote in 1918).

The basis for material progress was the improved state of the Welsh economy. The Napoleonic Wars (1799–1815) had increased demand for agricultural products, iron, and coal – which were among Carmarthenshire's greatest resources. Farmers saw the

Queen Victoria (Library of Congress, LC-USZ62-99500)

potential for higher profits if they could raise productivity and if road conditions improved so that food could be transported more quickly to market, so marginal land, such as woodland and uplands, was cultivated. Although Carmarthenshire remained essentially a rural county throughout the Victorian era, in places the landscape was radically changed. From Llanelli to Pembrey, there was a string of factories, power stations, mills and mines.

Many of the savageries unquestioned by previous generations had been abolished or curbed by the Victorians, including animal-baiting, public executions, flogging of soldiers and sailors and transportation. For the first time, people could drink beer from Llanelli breweries. Drink, however, caused its fair share of anxiety. In 1877, a local newspaper editor bemoaned:

> The Evil of the Day – That the present drinking customs of our youth are becoming truly appalling no-one can deny … the demoralisation brought about through the intermingling of the youth of both sexes in the smoky kitchens or back parlours of the 'pub'.

The Temperance movement was strong in Carmarthenshire. Members who joined a temperance society were required to 'take the pledge'. The Carmarthen pledge in 1836 included agreement to abstain from 'Distilled Spirits, Wine, Ale, Porter, Cider and all other intoxicating liquors' except for medicinal purposes or as part of a religious ceremony. Taking the pledge was a real test of character, given that home brewing and drinking was an intrinsic part of people's lives. Welsh farming communities took every opportunity to prepare home brew for weddings, funerals, pig-killing, harvest gatherings and other festivals. In Carmarthen alone, there were approximately 150 taverns in the nineteenth century which were 'open all hours' on market days. Yet people from all occupations joined the Temperance movement. The Carmarthen society included shoemakers, servants, policemen, printers, students, sailors and labourers. In the 1850s, seventy women and nineteen children were among more than 350 members. In Llanelli in 1882, more than 4,000 took part in a Great Temperance Demonstration to celebrate the closing of public houses on Sunday.

What kind of people would you have met if you walked around rural Carmarthenshire at the start of Queen Victoria's reign? We get a good idea from the 1841 Census returns. The parish of Llanfihangel Abercywyn, as an example, included farmers, agricultural labourers, publicans, a maltster, weaver, stonemason, shopkeeper, clog maker, merchant, butcher, shoemaker, miller, tailor, carpenter, blacksmith, horse-keeper, errand boy, lead miner, knitter of stockings, railway platelayer, station master, railway porter, toll-collector, cabinet maker, lawyer, mineral agent, auctioneer, land agent, cow-keeper and ploughboy.

However, the census was not the most accurate of sources. Many people held down more than one job at the same time. Teachers, for example, also worked as farmers. You would have also met dressmakers, bakers, rag-and-bone merchants, cattle dealers, drovers, cooks, saddlers, quilt makers, rat catchers, harness makers and pedlars. Much work was seasonal in nature. You would certainly encounter house servants, coal miners and those working in the iron industry – these were the three major employments in nineteenth-century Carmarthenshire.

The coming of the railways was to have a major impact on the social and economic life of people in the county. Prior to the railways, most folk had to walk to get to their destinations. No one was able to travel faster than a horse. Stagecoaches were slow, expensive and uncomfortable. But the railways changed how people saw the world. It had become a smaller place. Goods, services, ideas – and criminals – moved more rapidly. The boundary between town and country was increasingly blurred.

Although the first passengers in the world were carried on the Swansea–Mumbles line in 1807, it was not until 1852 that the South Wales railway extended to Carmarthen. On 17 September, up to 800 well-dressed passengers – accompanied by a military band – made the first train journey to the 'far west' from Swansea station. En route one of the carriages proved too wide and hit the side of Cwmbwrla tunnel, resulting in masonry falling on the lord lieutenant, his son and other passengers. Despite this inauspicious start, the railway opened up new worlds. Carmarthen was no longer dependent on the river or stagecoaches for trade and travel. In 1869 it was possible to reach London from Carmarthen in about seven hours via the new express train, calling at Llanelli, Swansea, Neath, Cardiff, Newport, Chepstow, Gloucester, Cheltenham, Swindon and Paddington.

Many of the county's public buildings date from the 1800s. These include schools, libraries, railway stations, museums, places of worship and pubs. Take Llanelli as an example. Very few of the town's pre-nineteenth century buildings survive, except for the tower of the parish church and Llanelly House opposite. The following were built in Llanelli during the nineteenth century:

- First Post Office – 1811
- Bryntirion Hospital (former workhouse) – 1837
- Llanelli Library – 1855–57
- Llanelli Railway Station – 1870s
- Old Road School – 1874–75
- Cwmlliedi Reservoir – 1878
- New Theatre – 1881
- Town Hall – 1894–96
- Parc Howard – 1882–86

Most of Llanelli's churches and chapels were built in the nineteenth century, including Baptist chapels in Marine Street and Cornish Place, Capel Als (Independent) in Wern Road, the Calvinistic Methodist chapels in Felinfoel Road and Lakefield Road, the Wesleyan chapel in Hall Street and the English Presbyterian chapel in Cowell Street. It is misleading to think of these chapels merely as buildings, they were the focal points for religious, social, cultural and educational activities. They offered everything from children's tea parties, singing festivals, annual excursions to the seaside, Sunday school classes, Band of Hope meetings, marches, processions, baptism ceremonies, and sermons from the pulpit that touched upon all aspects of life. At Capel Als in Llanelli, there were a number of extensions to accommodate a larger congregation. More than 800 attended sermons delivered by the energetic minister, David Rees, regarded by some as the best preacher in Wales.

CARMARTHENSHIRE
CHURCHES AND CHAPELS

St Peter's in Carmarthen is the oldest church in the county and
the largest in Wales with the capacity to seat up to 870 people.
The recorded history begins in the 1100s but it may have been built
on a much older Celtic site. The tower, nave and chancel are the oldest
parts of the present building, dating to the thirteenth century. Near the
chancel stands the tomb of Sir Rhys ap Thomas, who died in 1525.
He was a major player in the rise of Henry Tudor, who won the Battle
of Bosworth in 1485 to become King Henry VII. Rhys was knighted
for his loyal support and rewarded with vast estates. The church
also contains a memorial to Sir Richard Steele (1672–1729), who
was the first to publish modern periodicals in the form of *Tatler*
and *The Spectator*. Steele once said that 'reading was to the mind as
exercise is to the body'. His link with Carmarthen was through his
marriage to Mary Scurlock, from Llangunnor. There are also tablets to
commemorate Dr Robert Ferrar (d. 1555), the martyred Bishop of St
David's, and Sir William Nott (1782–1845), presented as Carmarthen's
most famous soldier.

The tomb of Rhys ap Thomas

Capel Als, Llanelli, is a Grade II listed building, first established by the Independents in 1780. The site was practically rebuilt in 1894. The preacher David Rees (1801–69) served as minister for forty years from 1829, and his Sunday night sermons typically attracted a congregation of around 850. He was nicknamed 'The Agitator' for his radical views.

St Elli parish church, Llanelli, is a Grade II listed building with a history going back to before the Norman Conquest and is associated with St Elli, a sixth-century Welsh saint. It has been restored many times.

St Teilo, Llandeilo, is another church dedicated to a Welsh saint, Teilo, who was a contemporary of St David. The present church is largely Victorian, built around 1850, aside from the late medieval tower. This was originally used as a lookout for approaching armies.

Soar y Mynydd is Wales' most remote chapel, surrounded by woodland on the road to Llyn Brianne. It was built in 1822 to meet the needs of hill farmers and drovers.

Bwlch y Rhiw, Cilycwm is another very remote chapel, located on the pass between the Cothi and Tywi valleys. The chapel was built in the early 1700s for Baptists.

St Ishmael's church, Ferryside, commands the most dramatic view from anywhere in Wales. It includes a sundial built into the wall, above the church door. In 2006, the grounds were developed to encourage biodiversity in churchyards.

St Margaret's church, Eglwys Gymyn, St Clears, has medieval foundations but major restoration occurred in 1900. A Latin and Ogham stone mentions Avitoria, 'daughter of Cynin' who lived in the fifth century. Cynin was an Irish chief, also called Brychan, who gave his name to Brecon. Just to confuse matters further, he is also referred to as Cymyn, Cummin, Gummin, Gymyn and the original Irish spelling Chummein. Inside the church on the wall is a mural of the Ten Commandments, part of which is said to date back to the 1300s.

St Mary's church, Kidwelly, is a Grade I listed building whose interior includes a rare carved fifteenth-century figure of the

Virgin Mary, set back in a niche. The oldest part of the church is its tower, which includes a stone spire more than 1,000 years old.

Holy Trinity church, Pontargothi, was built in 1865 on the order of H.J. Bath, a Swansea shipping magnate, who bought a house nearby at Llanegwad. He was annoyed to find that the only local church services available were in Welsh, so he decided to build his own church for English worshippers. Local folklore suggests that the path leading to the church was divided into two and made wide enough so that Bath and his wife could walk arm-in-arm separate from the servants, who walked in single file. Bath died just after the foundation stone was laid. The interior is very ornate and richly decorated, in contrast to the rather austere exterior.

CARMARTHENSHIRE POOR AND ITS WORKHOUSES

Despite incredible advances in material wealth for the middle classes during the Victorian period and a general increase in the standards of living, the majority of people in Carmarthenshire remained poor. It was common for families to be crowded into single rooms within lodging houses, a husband and wife sharing the same bed of filthy rags or straw with their four or five children. There was no running water or proper means of disposing of sewage, increasing the likelihood of disease and illness. Outbreaks of cholera, typhus, smallpox and scarlet fever were frequent. In 1847 the streets of Kidwelly were described as seldom swept, full of dung heaps and pigsties, with human waste thrown into open gutters.

It was reported in the early 1800s that the rural poor of Carmarthenshire lived in houses 'built of stone and mud, roofed with fern, reeds and turf, and were without chimneys; the doors were low; there were holes instead of windows, and these were often covered with wood filled with straw and rags'. In some cases, these deplorable conditions were still around at the end of the century. In 1899, David Davies was fined £1 5s for keeping a lodging house in St Catherine's Street where twenty men, women and children slept, when the registered maximum was ten.

When Queen Victoria died, the Mayor of Carmarthen announced that it had been a glorious reign, unprecedented in world history. As expected, the local newspaper columns, black-edged as a sign of respect, were quick to praise the 'good and great Queen' as the world united in mourning her death. As the Victorian era came to an end, many Carmarthenshire people were still struggling to achieve a comfortable life. For those who became destitute and could not afford to rent a room, they could sleep rough on the streets. Alternatively, and often as a final resort, the poor could enter one of the county's five workhouses.

These much-hated institutions had been set up to meet the widespread problem of poverty by getting the able-bodied 'inmates' back in work as soon as possible. In the late eighteenth century, a small workhouse had been established in Laugharne, but the Poor Law Amendment Act of 1834 introduced a new administrative unit for poor relief – the Poor Law Union, comprising a group of adjacent parishes. Five union workhouses were established, located in Carmarthen, Newcastle Emlyn, Llandovery, Llandeilo and Llanelli. Those deemed to be idiots, lunatics, blind, imbeciles, and deaf and dumb were among those admitted. Many entered the workhouses during times of particular hardship, such as the agricultural depression of the 1870s when farmers suffered from a series of bad harvests and competition from abroad that drove down their prices and hence their profits.

Peter Higginbotham's excellent website (www.workhouses.org.uk) provides information on each of these workhouses, including maps and a list of inmates as recorded in the 1881 Census returns. Among the residents of the Llanelli workhouse in 1881, for example, were 33-year-old Margaret Hopkins, a farmer's wife, and her three children, David (7), William (5) and Thomas (2), a 17-year-old imbecile called Betsy Edwards and 79-year-old widow Mary Thomas, who used to run a toyshop in Carmarthen. Workhouse conditions were not designed to be comfortable but they did provide basic food and shelter, which otherwise were beyond the means of those who entered. D.J. Evans, who worked as a porter at Carmarthen workhouse in the early 1930s, recalled that there was a good bakehouse where an inmate and his assistant baked huge loaves.

For breakfast and evening meal, each person received one slice of bread, 8oz in weight and over an inch thick, thinly spread with margarine, along with tea and cheese. Soup was the main course for dinner. On Sundays there was a piece of cake and on Saturday afternoons the inmates could go into town. There were occasional treats, and at Christmas the local brewery donated beer. In 2018 Carmarthen workhouse was heavily damaged by fire and remains in a poor state.

By the 1900s, reformers began to influence the government to move away from workhouses towards more specialised institutions. The language of the workhouse era began to change, with terms such as 'pauper' dropped and a gradual shift towards a more humane attitude to the less fortunate. The 1906 Liberal victory at the general election brought significant changes to Welsh society. For one thing, it marked the end of the gentry's dominance in the political running of Wales. Liberal politicians were largely drawn from lawyers, businessmen and entrepreneurs. New taxes were introduced as part of the 'People's Budget' of 1909 and a programme of welfare reforms began, including the introduction of free school meals, pensions for those aged over 70 and National Insurance, before the interruption of the First World War.

Carmarthen Civic Society campaigns to restore the town's old buildings and give them a new lease of life. For example, the Zion Methodist Chapel on Mansell Street is now a camera shop.

THROUGH THE WARS: 1914–50

The First World War, 1914–18
The year 2014 marked the 100th anniversary of the start of what was called the Great War. Films, books, magazines, documentaries and digital archives, such as Cymru 1914 (www.cymru1914.org), have brought all aspects of the war to the attention of researchers, students and the general public. The First World War touched almost every family and community in Carmarthenshire, as testified by war memorials from Abergorlech to Whitland.

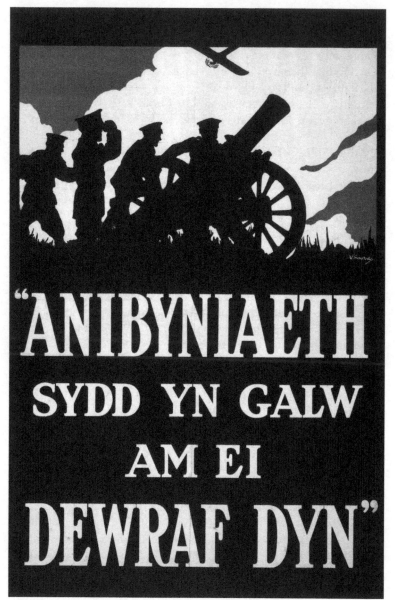

A Welsh First World War poster. It reads: 'Independence calls the bravest man'.
(Library of Congress, LC-USZC4-11037)

For the most part, the people of Carmarthenshire greeted the outbreak of the First World War with enthusiasm. Men joined the war for different reasons. For many, it was the sense of adventure. The fight on behalf of Belgium, unjustly invaded by Germany, was seen as a moral war – 'Truth, justice and freedom' was the rallying cry in the local newspapers. But not everyone in Carmarthenshire embraced the war. A few conscientious objectors appealed to local tribunals on grounds of religious belief, but these had little support.

Steven John's book *Carmarthen in the Great War* reveals some of the lesser-known stories of the First World War. One Carmarthen family received news that a son had been killed in Palestine; then, a few weeks later, the father and another son drowned in Llansteffan. On 8 February 1918 the body of Dominzo Mobilo, a Cardiff sailor, was washed ashore at Laugharne. Although he had managed to get off his ship and was wearing a lifebelt, he died before making it ashore. Another body, badly decomposed, was washed ashore in Llansteffan.

Understandably, the signing of the Armistice on 11 November at 11 a.m. (French time) in 1918 brought unsurpassed joy throughout Carmarthenshire. The celebrations in Ammanford were typical: the Silver Band played popular marching songs, children waved flags parading the streets, a holiday was granted to the miners and, as the local newspaper reported, 'everyone wore a smile'.

Unfortunately this did not last and the relief should not mask the deep-seated grief experienced by many, particularly girlfriends, wives and mothers. Juliet Nicholson describes 'the Great Silence' that befell the nation in 1918–20. Women faced the prospect of a single life or marrying beneath their station, given the shortage of suitable partners. The lack of a funeral also meant closure was very difficult for many women. In 1915 the army had decided not to return the bodies of officers and soldiers for burying, largely due to the numbers but also because so many were mutilated and unrecognisable.

While the wounded and limbless were noticeable, those who suffered from the newly diagnosed condition of 'shell shock' were less understood. A number of these men, 'absent in mind', were sent to the United Counties Lunatic Asylum in Carmarthen (built in 1865) suffering delusions and fits of anger or simply unable to communicate. They were 'treated' with electric shocks, drugs and warm baths, and occupational therapies such as basket weaving and painting. Their tragic stories deserve to be told but are beyond the scope of this little history. As well as coping with post-war traumas, the people of Carmarthenshire experienced their share of economic hardships during the 1920s and '30s.

War Memorials

Throughout Carmarthenshire there are memorials to military leaders and those who died in the various wars: Crimean (1853–56), Boer (1899–1902) and the two world wars. The West Wales Memorial website (www.wwwmp.co.uk) provides a great deal of information on these. It was established by Steven John to commemorate men and women from Carmarthenshire, Ceredigion and Pembrokeshire who have fallen in conflicts throughout the world. Inevitably, there is considerable coverage of the two world wars. The website includes details of individuals who demonstrated remarkable bravery, acknowledged by the award of the Victoria Cross (VC), the highest military honour. Those honoured came from different social classes. Among the gentlemen officers was John Vaughan Campbell, from Golden Grove, who was awarded the VC for his gallantry in leading his men during the Battle of the Somme in 1916. Lance Corporal William Fuller from Laugharne was awarded his VC for carrying a seriously wounded Captain Mark Haggard 100yds to a first-aid dressing station. William remained with Haggard until he died, his last words being 'Stick it, Welch.'

Carmarthen has war statues to commemorate the leadership of Sir William Nott (1782–1845) and Sir Thomas Picton (1758–1815). Although born in Neath and educated in Cowbridge, Sir William Nott looked upon Carmarthen as his home – his father was the landlord of the Ivy Bush. He joined the army in 1800 to serve in India and famously led a campaign in the Afghan Wars of 1842 before returning to Carmarthen, retiring on grounds of ill health. His statue was erected in Market Street (renamed Nott's Square) in 1851. It is made out of bronze, from guns captured at the Battle of Maharajpur. He is buried in St Peter's church.

Thomas Picton, born in Haverfordwest, was a general in the Napoleonic Wars and in 1815 became the most senior officer to die at the Battle of Waterloo. One report suggests he was shot through the head by a French rifleman. According to family tradition, however, he was shot by one of his own men who hated him. Regardless of how he died, Picton is seen as a national hero for his courage, one of the twelve 'Heroes of Wales' commemorated with a marble statue in Cardiff. Newspapers described him as the greatest soldier Wales has produced since Owain Glyndŵr and he remains the only Welshman buried in St Paul's Cathedral. However, there was a dark side to his character. While he was Governor of Trinidad, he was convicted for ordering the illegal torture of Louisa Calderón, the mistress of a Spanish merchant. She was suspended from a pulley set in the roof of a torture cell, and then lowered on to a sharpened spike set in the floor. Picton's lawyers managed to secure a retrial at which the legality of the torture, although deplored, was accepted under Spanish law. The Duke of Wellington regarded Picton 'a rough foulmouthed devil as ever lived, but he always behaved extremely well; no man could do better in different services I assigned to him'.

The Picton Monument has had a pretty disastrous history. It took more than a decade to raise the necessary funds before the original 75ft monument was erected in 1828. The decorative features soon weathered and by 1846 the statue had to be taken down. Replacement sculptures were made but forgotten about until the 1970s, when they were transferred to the County Museum. Meanwhile, a new statue was put in place in 1847 but this became unsafe and in the 1980s rebuilt stone by stone on more solid foundations. A time capsule from the original monument, containing Picton's Waterloo medal and other coins, was removed for display in the County Museum. In 2020, a public vote decided to keep the Picton Monument in Carmarthen, despite Picton's links to the slave trade. The vote followed the global Black Lives Matters protests around all aspects of racial inequality. 1613 voters said no action was needed and 744 suggested removing the statue to another location, such as Carmarthen Museum, destroying it or erecting an information board.

Crimean War cannon at work (Library of Congress, LC-DIG-ppmsca-05698)

Lammas Street, Carmarthen, contains the Crimean War statue in memory of the soldiers and officers from the 23rd Royal Welch Fusiliers who died in the war with Russia. The names of individuals who fell in combat at the battles of Alma, Redan, Inkerman and Sebastopol are listed. Many more died of disease – 526 non-commissioned officers, drummers and private soldiers. The regiment's Colonel Lysons and officers paid for the monument. Originally a captured Russian gun appeared before the monument but was later removed. A company of the regiment was the first British force to land on Crimean soil.

In Guildhall Square, there is a memorial to the thirty-two men who died in the South African War (Boer War). It takes the form of an officer in Boer War campaign dress. Originally there was a captured Boer cannon in front of the memorial. Among those listed is Lieutenant William Arthur Glanmor Williams, from Ferryside, who joined the South Wales Borderers in 1893. He died in 1900 at the age of 27, attempting to save his colonel who had come under sniper fire at Bothaville in the Orange Free State. In 1905, thousands gathered in heavy rain to witness the unveiling of the Boer War statue in Llanelli by Earl Roberts, the former Commander-in-Chief in South Africa. The monument can be seen in the Town Hall grounds.

Officially, the Carmarthen County War Memorial commemorates the loss of 1,913 lives during the First World War: 123 officers, 254 non-commissioned officers, three nurses and 1,533 other ranks. However, further research by the West Wales War Memorial Project has revised this to around 2,700, a figure likely to increase following further research. Many Carmarthenshire men fell at the major battles at Ypres and the Somme; on 15 July 1916, twelve men lost their lives during the initial assault while a further fifty Carmarthen men fell during the second attack three days later. Among those named on the Kidwelly War Memorial are three brothers: David, Samuel and William Hughes, who were all killed in less than a year of each other

In 2019, a plaque was unveiled at Carmarthen railway station in honour of the eight railway workers who died in World War One.

Interwar Years

The years between the two world wars have generally been treated with great pessimism in Wales. This was a time of economic depression, mass unemployment, endemic poverty and the rapid spreading of fatal diseases such as tuberculosis. It is hard to escape images of soup kitchens, hunger marches and dole queues, diseased and near-starving families. The global economic troubles of the mid-1920s had a devastating impact on ordinary families. The South Wales coal industry suffered a sharp decline in demand caused by increased coal production elsewhere, the change to oil and the high exchange rate of sterling. Unemployment among coalminers rose from 2 per cent in April 1924 to 28.5 per cent in August 1925. By the early 1930s, unemployment in South Wales had reached 42 per cent and the region was among the most depressed in the world. Although those in the coal industry took the brunt, farmers also suffered, along with those working in steel, tinplate and transport. James Griffiths, elected MP for Llanelli in 1939, pointed out to Parliament that Burry Port experienced an unemployment rate of 85 per cent during the 1920s and 1930s following the decision to close the Royal Ordnance Factory despite promises to keep it open after the war. The factory was sold for scrap and left in ruins, but during the Second World War another factory was built on the site.

In 1930, the *Llanelli Mercury* declared 'no cause for optimism' when 350 men lost their jobs at the steel works, blaming foreign competition.

Mass emigration occurred, with 390,000 Welsh people leaving the country in search of a better life. The government introduced a means test to reduce unemployment benefits to families who had other income, but this was widely condemned for its intrusiveness and insensitive handling, resulting in mass protests in 1935. Working-class families resorted to various means of keeping their heads above water: some kept chickens or pigs, cobbled shoes, repaired clothes, picked coal, grew food on allotments and did 'odd jobs' for small payments, while children collected blackberries and other wild fruits or ran errands for a few pence. In Llanelli a Mayor's Shilling Fund was set up to provide children with boots and clothes, with lists of donors published in local newspapers. Not everyone appreciated the council and charitable offers of support. Thomas Evans, aged 58, from Tumble, wrote to the editor of the *Llanelli Mercury* to complain about 'the miles of red tape' in applying for relief. Although he had received underclothes and boots from the Lord Mayor's Fund, the boots were of such poor quality they disintegrated on the first wet day. Although active, he had been unemployed for three years and told that he was too old to work in the colliery. He could not understand how unemployed men in the neighbouring parish of Llanarthney had been granted 'a cartload of goods' when he could not even get a pair of boots to 'genuinely seek work'.

Although it is wrong to underestimate the struggles faced by many working-class families in Carmarthenshire during the 1920s and 1930s, living standards for those in work actually rose during the interwar period. New consumer goods were advertised in newspapers such as the *Carmarthen Journal* and *Llanelli Mercury* and became available for those families who could afford to buy them. For example, the Llanelli Electrical Company offered free home demonstrations to housewives on exactly how its new vacuum cleaner differed from all other cleaners, putting an end to beating carpets out of doors. The company had no doubts over the appeal of its product:

Wait till You Try the New Hoover
It is unquestionably the finest cleaner that has ever come on the market. Amazingly efficient – thorough, quick and, above all, astoundingly easy to handle. The New Hoover is a piece of superb engineering skill.

These years were not all doom and gloom. John Edwards, author of *Llanelli: Story of a Town*, recalled growing up in the town during the 1930s:

> Life was quite pleasant. The old market was a magical place with its variety of stalls. There were beautiful shops, which sold everything that any heart could desire. Fish-and-chip shops provided wholesome fare and Italian cafés served ice cream and coffee among other delights. The YMCA proved a haven of rest and relaxation with a beautifully furnished lounge and snooker room. Concerts were held regularly, mainly in chapels, and we were given the opportunity of seeing and hearing world-famous singers performing solo roles in oratorios. Most of us were poor but we did not realise it because everyone else was in the same boat.

A scan through newspaper adverts of the time give a flavour of how people entertained themselves during these difficult days.

The *Llanelli Mercury* shows on 30 April 1931:

- Llanelli Cinema in Stepney Street showing Gary Cooper and Mary Brian in the 'thrilling adventure-romance' *Only the Brave*, describing the stars as 'the sweetest sweethearts on the screen'.
- Hippodrome, Llanelli's Talking House, offered a week of Tom Walls' 'witty and sparkling dialogue and brilliant acting in a delightful comedy' with cheap prices available up to 3.45 p.m.
- GWR Cheap Trips from Llanelli with bookings from surrounding stations.
- A free public lecture on 'A Righteous Government' by Mr F. Chester.
- Maison Beattie's Ladies' Hairdressing and Permanent Waving Specialists in Market Street.
- H.G. Sage and Son's Luxury Sunshine Coaches, from Burry Port.

During the 1930s, one of the traditions among miners' families from South Wales was to go on holiday to Llansteffan during the last week of July and the first week of August. This was known as 'miner's fortnight'. Sun, sea and sand provided respite from the toil of working underground. The families would catch the train to Ferryside and then take the ferry across to Llansteffan beach.

The Second World War

South-west Wales was at the forefront of preparations for the Second World War. Its position and distance from the Continent meant that it was ideally placed to train personnel, manufacture and store armaments, test weapons and carry out research. Defending the West Wales coastline was critical in the battle for the Atlantic and to avert a possible invasion of Germany via Ireland. In 1940, a Ministry of Defence research base opened at Pendine, and the nearby Morfa Bychan beach was used for rehearsals for the D-Day landings. The remains of battery and lookouts can be seen along the coastline, for example at St Ishmael's. The authorities established a defensive line to the west of Carmarthen, made up of anti-tank ditches and pillboxes.

The term 'home front' summed up the prevailing view that civilians could make a valuable contribution to the war effort, for instance by producing armaments and munitions. In July 1940, the munitions factory at Burry Port was among the first of the industrial targets to suffer from enemy bombing. Ten workers were killed and a large number were injured.

Evacuees

The government was fully aware that German planes would target cities such as London, Manchester, Bristol and Swansea, and casualties were likely to be high. Their evacuation scheme was a remarkable response. Those considered to be most vulnerable – schoolchildren and teachers, mothers with children under the age of 5, and disabled people – were moved by train out of the cities to the countryside, where there was little risk of bombing raids. Around 10,000 children were evacuated to Carmarthenshire, mostly from Liverpool and London. In September 1939, more than 1,000 evacuees from Liverpool, on board three trains, were welcomed at Llanelli railway station. Unfortunately the last Liverpool train did not arrive until after 10 p.m., by which point a 'Black-Out Order' was in force. This meant the station and streets were in complete darkness, which added to the 'hysteria' among the arriving children and babies.

These months were known as 'the phoney war' and many had returned home by Christmas because no threat materialised. Nonetheless, a further 1,100 London evacuees arrived in Llanelli in June 1940.

The blackout lasted from 1 September 1939, two days before war was declared, to 23 April 1945. To minimise the risk of German bombing, all streetlights were switched off at the mains, vehicle headlights were masked to show only a crack of light, and police stations were lit by candles. Wardens checked for compliance and some people were prosecuted for ignoring warnings. While the blackout may have protected lives from German bombings, it also led to an increase in road deaths as motorists struggled to adjust to restricted lighting. Coroners urged pedestrians to carry a white handkerchief or newspaper to make them more visible.

The evacuation led to lasting friendships. But there was also friction. Some Llanelli people grumbled about the coarse habits and bad language of city children. A senior police officer in Carmarthen complained that female evacuees and war workers from England were 'teaching local women to drink'. Welsh-speaking hosts with little command of English struggled to communicate with their visitors. There were new sights and sounds on both sides. For many rural Carmarthenshire folk, this was the first time they heard people with Cockney or Scouse accents or saw black men when Americans were stationed in Pembrokeshire. The soldiers came with supplies of food, gum, stockings and money to spend in the pubs, which increased their popularity amongst children and young women eager to follow American fashions. Some evacuees found it difficult to adjust to the green fields, woods, rivers and lanes of the Carmarthenshire countryside and missed the buzz of the city. In Ferryside, near Carmarthen, Londoners apparently refused to leave their bus because the village was too quiet.

The Second World War had some unusual consequences. In 1941, the villagers of Cil-y-Cwm had a windfall when a wealthy local landowner, Ivor Campbell Davys, sold his Neuadd Fawr estate and all the surrounding farms because he thought the Germans were about to invade. They did not and those that bought the properties did very well.

Prisoner-of-War Camps

A number of prisoner-of-war camps were established during 1940–41. Two were set up in Carmarthen, at Johnstown and Glangwilli. Another was built at Henllan near Llandysul on the Ceredigion/Carmarthenshire border, to hold mainly Italian prisoners in 1943–46. The dene (valley) consisted of around thirty-five huts to house the prisoners, a theatre, kitchen, hospital and bathing facilities. In May 1943, around 1,200 Italians captured in Libya and Tunisia were marched from the local train station to the camp. Many were allowed to work on local farms in northern Carmarthenshire, where they were well received. Mario Ferlito, a 21-year-old prisoner, took the lead in converting one of the huts into a Catholic church; he painted a fresco showing the Last Supper on the wall behind the altar and other frescos on walls and roof beams. The prisoners made their own paint from fruit such as strawberries and elderberries, red cabbage and fish oil from tinned sardines. The altar was made from pieces of wood recycled from Red Cross parcels and candlesticks constructed from food tins such as bully beef tins. The church was named 'The Church of the Sacred Heart'. In 1946, around 700 of the prisoners were repatriated to Italy, while around fifty chose to stay and settled in the area, marrying Welsh girls. Although German prisoners were then received, the camp closed in 1947. Ferlito returned with fifteen others to see their church in 1977 at the request of local schoolchildren. He made regular visits to Wales where he established many friendships, before his death in 2009 at the age of 86.

KEY DATES

c. **40,000** BC	Earliest evidence of human life in Carmarthenshire at Coygan Cave
c. **600** BC	Iron Age hill forts
c. AD **75**	The Romans build a fort at Carmarthen known as Moridunum
383	Roman withdrawal of troops from Wales
547	Plague sweeps through the region

852	First recorded attack by the Vikings in South Wales
940	Codification of the laws of Wales, by Hywel Dda
1093	Norman Conquest of Wales begins with death of Rhys ap Tewdwr
1095	First Norman castle built in Wales, at Rhyd y Gors, on banks of River Tywi in Carmarthen
1184	Talley Abbey founded
1284	Carmarthen made first county town in Wales
1349	Black Death hits Carmarthenshire
1567	New Testament translated into Welsh by Bishop Morgan at Bishop's Palace, Abergwili
1576	Queen Elizabeth Grammar School founded in Carmarthen
1602	George Owen of Henllys describes Carmarthen, the largest town in Wales, as 'fair and good in state'
1718	First legal printing press in Wales established at Adpar near Newcastle Emlyn
1763	John Wesley preaches in Carmarthen and visits Llanelli and Llandeilo in the 1770s
1766–68	Kymer Canal built
1783	First recorded cricket match played in Wales at Court Henry Down, Carmarthenshire
1810	*Carmarthen Journal*, the oldest surviving newspaper in Wales, first published
1836	First police force established in Carmarthen
1837	Llanelli cricket club founded, the oldest in South Wales
1839–43	Rebecca riots
1840	Llanelly Pottery established
1848	South Wales and Monmouthshire Training College (now University of Wales Trinity Saint David) the oldest provider of teacher training in Wales, is established
1852	South Wales railway reaches Carmarthen
1865	Joint Counties Lunatic Asylum opened in Carmarthen
1875	Llanelli Rugby Club formed
1884	Ten die in Garnant Colliery Disaster (Amman Valley) when the rope of their cage break and they fall 219ft
1923	Closure of Llanelli Pottery
1936/37	RAF Pembrey opened
1940	Henllan Bridge Farm Prisoner of War Camp built

1947	First Welsh medium school opened by a local education authority, Ysgol Dewi Sant in Llanelli
1950	Carmarthen Bay Electrical Generating Station opened (and demolished in 1991)
1951	Closure of North Dock, Llanelli
1952–56	Trostre steelworks (Llanelli) built
1954	Ronnie Harris executed at Swansea prison, the last man hanged in Wales. He was kept at St Clears police station after being found guilty of murdering John and Phoebe Harries the previous year
1954	Ronnie Harries, a married farmhand from Pendine, was convicted of double murder. He became the last man to be executed in Wales.
1963	Beeching Report on railways leads to closures of stations and lines such as Carmarthen to Aberystwyth (1965)
1966	Gwynfor Evans becomes first Plaid Cymru Member of Parliament
1972	Llanelli beat the New Zealand All Blacks, 9–3
1980	Pembrey Country Park opened
1984	Hywel Dda Memorial Gardens opened
1984–85	Miners' strike
1988	Industrial Museum opened in Kidwelly
1990	First wind farm to generate electricity in Wales opened in Carmarthen Bay
1991	Wildfowl and Wetlands Centre opened at Penclacwydd, Bynea
1995	Millennium Coastal Park project begins
2000	National Botanic Garden opened
2005	Restoration of Llanelly House begins (completed in 2013)
2010	In December, the river Towy froze over for the first time since 1940, while Pendine village had a frozen sea edge
2014	Welsh television channel S4C announces headquarters to be located in Carmarthen
2021	Major plans announced to redevelop Llanelli, including a new Wellness and Life Science Village
2021	A new drive-through mass vaccination centre opened at the Carmarthen Showground in the wake of the coronavirus pandemic

3

RIOTS AND REBELS, CRIMES AND PUNISHMENTS

These days Carmarthen may be seen as a quiet market town but this has not always been the case. In 1603, George Owen described it as having 'many unruly and querulous people' while robberies, brawling and 'other disorders' were common throughout the county. Carmarthenshire has been billed 'the wild west' for good reasons. It has a long history of violence, social unrest and protest. But another way to look at the history of the county is to celebrate the determination of ordinary people to stand up for justice and what they believed to be right.

CARMARTHEN RIOTS, 1740–64

In the eighteenth century, Carmarthen town was the most turbulent in Wales. Politics was a violent business. The town had two mayors and two common councils, both of which had their own gangs fighting each other. Elections led to disturbances of the peace – in 1740, a labourer shot one of the election agents. In 1755 a frightened sheriff wrote to Parliament declaring that he expected 'the town in flames every minute', armed mobs of around 500 wandered the streets. In December, a bookseller died of his wounds. Some rent collectors were too fearful to enter the town.

The people themselves were not slow to air their grievances. In the 1750s, Carmarthen councillors were told to stop enclosing common land that the poor were using for grazing their animals and for collecting firewood. Threats were even made to tear out the hearts of councillors in Carmarthen and feed them to the dogs. No wonder then that Carmarthen in the 1750s has been likened to the mafia-controlled Chicago of the 1920s.

FOOD RIOTS, 1818

Carmarthen was disturbed by food riots in 1800, 1818, 1829–30 and 1830–31. In 1818 a mob, led by a drum and fife band, prevented the export of cheese on a boat, which planned to sail from Carmarthen. These food riots occurred during times of hardship when people struggled to survive on little or no wages due to high unemployment and a slump in agriculture. They protested about the cost of bread and grain.

CARMARTHEN RIOTS, 1831

Red Street and Blue Street in Carmarthen town have their origins in the Red and Blue political parties of the eighteenth century. Different gentry families who competed for control of the borough led these – George Talbot Rice, Lord Dynevor, led the Reds, while the Blues were led by the Campbells, Barons Cawdor.

At a political meeting at the Guildhall during the 1831 elections, one of the opposition candidates got up on to the stage and began fighting with his opponent. This caused a riot that lasted three days. Special constables were assaulted; one man who entered the town to join the victory parade was dragged from his horse and beaten up for supporting the Reds, whose flag was torn from St Peter's church.

The incidents at Carmarthen took place against a backdrop known as the Reform Crisis (1830–32). The Whig party introduced the Reform Act in 1832 to address widespread electoral abuses. Although the system in Wales was less corrupt than that in England, bribery was common and private arrangements between wealthy families generally determined candidates for elections. Carmarthen reformers threatened to stop paying taxes if the Bill was defeated.

They disliked the Tories and in 1832 they ceremoniously burned the *Carmarthen Journal*, a Church and Tory newspaper, in the streets of the town. They greeted the passing of the Reform Act with great joy with church bells ringing and parades held on the streets.

Even after the Reform Bill was passed, Carmarthen remained a hotbed for radicalism and was regarded as the most dangerous town in Wales. The situation became unmanageable and so a police force was established in 1836, one of the first in Wales. By 1857 there were twelve constables, known locally as the 'Carmarthen Shilling'.

REBECCA RIOTS, 1839–43

Poverty was widespread in rural Carmarthenshire during the 1800s. Farmers had had enough of being exploited so, in 1839, they formed a protest movement known as 'Rebecca and her daughters'. One possible explanation for their name is that Rebecca may have been the name of the woman who lent her clothes to one of the ringleaders, Thomas Rees, to disguise his appearance. But these were people brought up on the Bible and they probably took the name

Rebecca riots, 1843 (10087385, *Illustrated London News*, Mary Evans Picture Library)

from a passage in Genesis where Rebecca talks of the need to destroy the gates of 'them that hate thee' (Genesis 24: 60). The enemies were the businessmen who formed companies known as Turnpike Trusts, which maintained roads in return for tolls. In practice, some agents were more interested in making money than keeping the roads in a good state. Although road conditions generally improved, farmers faced the prospect of paying several tolls to different companies over a short journey. It could cost as much as 5s (the equivalent of around £11 today) in tolls to move a cart of lime, needed as fertiliser, 8 miles inland. There were eleven tollgates around Carmarthen town alone.

At the height of the troubles, not a single tollgate was left standing in West Wales. All of this naturally alarmed the authorities. They regarded 'Rebecca and her daughters' as terrorists who attacked property and intimidated individuals, including those guilty of sexual misdemeanours, and greedy landowners. Even the 'fat Steward' and 'the old Bum' of a bailiff at Middleton Hall (Llanarthney) were threatened for collecting rents. The violence began when the tollgate at Efailwen, on the road leading from Narberth to Cardigan, was destroyed on 13 May 1839 and again in June and July. Then there was a pause in action until October 1842, when it was confined to the area between Narberth and St Clears. By spring 1843 it had spread to the Teifi Valley and to the district of Llanelli in the summer. A letter from the estate manager at Middleton Hall described the scene at Llanddarog tollhouse:

> A poor man who had offended them was last week dragged from his bed to the toll house which had been partly rebuilt – he was made to help them pull it down, by two saws held across his bare neck – he had no clothes but his shirt – his wife followed him to the last, half dressed and screaming – they made him walk towards his house on his bare knees and flogged him with a Cart Whip – all within sight of his house.

By then, a force of 1,800 soldiers had been sent to West Wales to curb the riots. On 7 September 1843, the only known fatality occurred. The tollgate keeper at Hendy, Sarah Williams, had been warned that the rioters were on their way but refused to leave. She was heard to cry 'I know who you are' by a family living up the road who had locked their doors from the rioters. The tollhouse was set alight and Williams called on a neighbour for help, but when she returned a shot was heard. She managed to struggle back to the neighbour's house but collapsed at the doorway and died. Incredibly at her inquest, despite several shot marks on her body, the cause of death was said to be unknown. There was a general feeling of hatred towards Sarah Williams as a toll collector, which might explain the verdict.

Although the Hendy tollhouse has disappeared, a small commemorative plaque has been erected on the village green. Tollgate houses can still be seen in Carmarthen at the bottom of Job's Well Road and on the Pontyberem approach entering the village of Llannon. A couple of the ringleaders from Five Roads were convicted and transported to Australia. The government agreed to investigate the reasons for the riots and its fair minded report led to legislation to improve the road network.

TITHE WARS, 1888

For centuries, people were expected to pay a tenth of their income to the Church in the form of tithes. Usually these payments were made in kind: wool, milk, crops or other produce. However, chapelgoers resented paying tithes to a church that they did not attend and tensions escalated following the agricultural depression that began in the 1870s. Many refused to pay the tithe and during the 1880s, the authorities resorted to the enforced sales of possessions to collect the taxes owed. This led to confrontations at the sales.

In 1888 Thomas Jones, a leading Nonconformist minister at Whitland, had not paid the tithe for two years. Angry crowds gathered when the bailiff, protected by constables, moved in to acquire three stacks of hay and a rick of corn (valued at £50 when the outstanding tithe was for £14). The auctioneer was nervous. The news reporter from Cardiff described a crowd which rose in number to around 500, equipped with 'tin pans, cracked kettles and cow horns'. These included 'rosy-cheeked Buxom Carmarthenshire lasses' and 'strong, broad shouldered brawny armed fellows' in the prime of life. It took the intervention of the local MP to pacify the crowd.

TUMBLE RIOTS, 1893, 1906

In September 1893, tensions between the managers and workers in the Great Mountain Colliery, Tumble, resulted in strike action. Soldiers and police were called in when forty or so strikers swept through Tumble, 'striking terror into the hearts of those who opposed them' (according to the local newspaper).

In the summer of 1906 there were further riots, forcing the Chief Constable to draw up plans for a police station to be built at Cross Hands. A crowd of around 100 pursued a police constable, who had arrested two brothers involved in a brawl at the Tumble Inn. They forced the release of the men by smashing the windows of the policeman's house. He did not have the luxury of the Glamorgan force, where all the police stations were connected via telephone so that assistance could be called for in the event of any disturbance.

The period from 1906–14 is called the Great Unrest, characterised by industrial conflicts throughout Britain and the growth of the Suffragette movement campaigning for women's rights.

LLANELLI RIOTS, 1911

The bloodiest conflict in twentieth-century Britain occurred in Llanelli in 1911. The railwaymen's strike had started on the afternoon of Thursday 17 August 1911, in protest at average wages of £1 per week. The pay was around 20 per cent below the average for skilled manual workers at the time. Better-paid colliers and tinplate workers joined up with the railwaymen, who blockaded Llanelli's two level crossings and stopped trains from passing. Thomas Jones, a local Justice of the Peace and shareholder in the Great Western Railway, called for assistance. Winston Churchill ordered in the troops. One striker shouted in Welsh: '*Popeth yn iawn! Blanc yw hi, bois! Peidiwch a symud, Saethan nhw ddim*' ('It's all right! It's blank, boys! Don't move, they won't shoot!'). Unfortunately he was wrong and two young men, John 'Jac' John and Leonard Worsell, were killed. Worsell was an innocent bystander who had simply come into the back garden, mid-shave, to see what all the commotion had been about.

The strikers responded by attacking shops, train trucks, the railway station and the town hall. Thomas Jones' grocer's shop was a particular target. When the rioters set fire to a freight wagon in sidings, they did not know that it contained explosive detonators. Four people were killed as a result. Ironically, behind closed doors, a deal had been agreed, brokered by the chairman of the board of trade, David Lloyd George, to end the strike.

The riots were not spoken about for many years. Local historian John Edwards believed that a conspiracy of silence between the local Liberal party and the chapels promoted a sense of shame about the events.

SCHOOL STRIKES, 1911

The year 1911 was one of industrial action throughout the UK. One of the lesser-known national strikes began at Bigyn Primary School in Llanelli on 5 September 1911. The trigger point was reported to have been when the deputy head punished a boy for passing a piece of paper around the class urging his peers to protest. Boys (there is no record of girls joining the strike) from different schools in the town emulated their fathers by taking to the streets, painting banners, organising meetings and picketing any 'scabs' that entered the school gates. Within days, the strikes had spread to sixty-two towns throughout the UK. Although they were soon quashed, teachers were increasingly held to account for their conduct and excessive use of corporal punishment, although the cane was not outlawed in state schools until 1986 and lingered on in the independent sector until 1998.

INDUSTRIAL STRIKES, 1918–19, 1926

Industrial action continued in Carmarthenshire during the interwar period. During 1919, teachers, farmers, tailors and roadmen were among those who protested about salaries, high prices, government policies or working conditions. The weavers of Drefach had a history of industrial action – they went out on strike over pay in 1873, 1880, 1883, 1891 and 1903. The most famous strike of the interwar years, the Great Strike of 1926, affected coalminers, railwaymen, bus and train drivers, and many others in Carmarthenshire's workforce.

CYMDEITHAS YR IAITH, 1960s–'80s

Over a twenty-year period, some 1,000 members of the Welsh language society Cymdeithas Yr Iaith were prosecuted for their campaign to raise the status of Welsh. Their well-publicised activities included daubing English-only road signs in paint, climbing television masts and refusing to pay bills issued only in English. Although committed to non-violent protest, more militant activists burned second holiday homes belonging to English families. In terms of convictions, the campaign represents one of the largest protest movements since the Suffragettes. The Welsh Language Act (1993) declared that Welsh should be treated on the same basis as English in public life, but this did not include private business. In 2004, eleven activists raided Radio Carmarthenshire's studios to protest against the lack of Welsh on the local airwaves – only 5 per cent of broadcast material was said to be in Welsh, while 50 per cent of the population were Welsh speakers. Such pressure groups contributed to changes in legislation in 2010–11, which put Welsh and English on par in both the public and private worlds.

MINERS' STRIKE, 1984–85

Carmarthenshire's coal industry effectively came to an end with the national miners' strike of 1984–85, during the premiership of Margaret Thatcher. The protracted dispute had a devastating impact on the coal communities of the Amman and Gwendraeth valleys. Deep-seated tensions developed between those who remained on strike and those who went back to work, as occurred at Cynheidre. Nearly forty years later, some ex-miners are still not on speaking terms. Those who returned to work felt that they had no option if they were to support their families.

Some men acted as 'flying pickets', travelling to various coalmines around Britain as well as visiting London to lobby Parliament. There was a strong camaraderie among the miners forged at centres such as the Ammanford Miner's Welfare Hall.

When Margaret Thatcher died in 2013, there were few tears shed in the former coal communities of Carmarthenshire.

COCKLE WARS, 1993

In June 1993, the sleepy village of Ferryside made national headlines. Professional pickers from Deeside in North Wales arrived on the beach to take advantage of a rare bumper crop of cockles. They clashed with locals, resulting in six men being injured. On one day, more than 40 tons of the shellfish were harvested at an average price of £10 per hundredweight (equivalent to an income of around £8,000).

CARMARTHEN GAOL

The most imposing building when approaching Carmarthen is the County Hall, once the location of the town's gaol. There is evidence of a gaol in Carmarthen dating back to 1532, when a monk named Dan Rychard was arrested and imprisoned for coining money in the monastery. The castle was converted into the county gaol in 1789 and later extended. The gaol closed in 1922 and little remains following demolition work in the 1930s to make way for the County Hall. The architect of the gaol, John Nash, who also designed Buckingham Palace and the Brighton Pavilion, had succeeded where mighty Welsh princes such as Llewelyn the Great and Owain Glyndŵr had previously failed.

During the nineteenth century, prisoners were employed on the tread wheel, which supplied water to the gaol. It has been estimated that a prisoner would typically spend six hours on the tread wheel each day, with five minutes' rest every quarter of an hour. Working morning and afternoon sessions, prisoners had to keep moving to maintain their position – by the end of the day they amassed the equivalent of 2,193ft per hour and climbed over 9,000ft, twice the height of Ben Nevis. They also broke stones for surrounding roads, cleaned bricks, sewed, made clogs and mended clothes. There were eight cells in the gaol, as well as a day room and exercise yard.

Those convicted of serious crimes – such as smuggling, stealing and murder – faced the death sentence. The guilty were hung on Babel Hill (Pensarn) and then placed in a gibbet in public view as a warning to others. *The Gentleman's Magazine* of May 1742 reported the case of an 8-year-old girl who had been acquitted at the Carmarthen Assize of murdering her two siblings, aged 6 and 4. The family lived in a cottage by the sea and had been told stories of Spanish cruelty and possible invasion. One day during a thunderstorm, when they happened to be alone, they became so terrified that the girl tried to kill herself using a hedge-cutting blade. At that moment her younger brother and sister cried out 'Pray sister, kill us first', which she did before wounding herself. Neighbours stopped her from throwing herself in the river.

However, pressure from humanitarian reformers meant that by 1837 capital punishment was only exercised for fifteen offences, including murder, treason and piracy; in the 1700s, people could be hanged for over 200 offences. The spectacle of a public hanging attracted much interest and hundreds of men, women and children would follow the last words and movements of the condemned. A new public gallows was erected inside the front wall of the county gaol facing Spilman Street where, in 1829, the last public execution took place. Around 10,000 gathered to see the execution of David Evans, who had confessed to the murder of his lover, Hannah Davies. However, on the execution day he believed that his life would be spared when the suspension apparatus gave way as he approached the drop. In broken English, he pleaded with those on the platform: 'No! No! Gentleman, was no hang twice for the same thing.'

He pleaded again in Welsh, but to no avail. His body was left hanging for an hour and then dissected and placed in a coffin, left open to public viewing.

A rare view of the criminal underworld is afforded through the photographic register of criminals or felons who passed through Carmarthen gaol between 1844 and 1870. The record is due to the efforts of the warden, who had an amateur interest in photography. It should be noted that the entries in the register are not completely reliable – prisoners gave false names and addresses, while those who were convicted may not necessarily have been guilty. The register and photographs can be viewed online at: www.welshlegalhistory.org/carms-felons-register.php. Here are some examples:

Anne Davies (aged 30) – unknown origin – 30 June 1848 – acquitted of unlawfully milking a cow

Harriet Lewis (aged 26) – from Llanddarog – 29 May 1851 – acquitted of attempting to murder her illegitimate son by smothering him under hay and clods of earth

Richard Vivian (aged 26) – from Llanelli – 13 March 1861 – seven days' hard labour for stealing cricket balls

John Evans (aged 14) – from Llanelli – 6 July 1864 – found guilty of attempting to steal strawberries and sentenced to fourteen days' hard labour and three years at a reformatory school

John Caveller (aged 40) – from Dublin – 24 September 1870 – found guilty of stealing a shoe and sentenced to two months' hard labour

The most widely reported case was that of the manslaughter of Sarah Jacob. Sarah was born in 1857 in the village of Llanfihangel ar arth, the third of seven children of Evan Jacob, a tenant farmer, and his wife, Hannah. Sarah was a bright child who suffered a mysterious illness (possibly viral encephalitis) in the spring of 1867. Despite being attended to by doctors, she stopped eating and soon became known as 'The Welsh Fasting Girl'. Her story attracted many tourists – the railway station at Pencader even had a specially built refreshment booth to accommodate the interest. One doctor who examined Sarah on her bed claimed that she was deceiving her simple parents and hid food in various drawers and cupboards. She would have been easily cured if admitted to a hospital. After two years' fasting, her death at Christmas 1869 made national headlines in *The Times*. At the inquest both parents were found guilty of neglect – the father was sentenced to a year in Swansea prison and the mother received six months.

Looting was a periodical problem associated with shipwrecks along the Carmarthenshire coastline. Gangs of looters would try to entice the ships on to the sands using false beacon fires. One gang was called 'Gwyr y Bwyell Bach', the men with the small hatchets. These weapons were used to chop off the fingers of victims to get the rings off and also break the casks of brandy and fine wine.

There have been around 380 shipwrecks on Cefn Sidn Sands, of which only a handful are visible. Following major storms in early 2014, ghostly shipwrecks emerged – having been buried by 30ft sand dunes – only to disappear again.

In December 1833, J.H. Rees, a Llanelli magistrate, notified the Home Office that, following the wreck on Cefn Sidan Sands of the 370-ton barque *Brothers* bound from Bahia (Brazil) to Liverpool, he could not prevent local farmers from plundering her cargo. This included 2,000 bales of cotton and 400 buffalo hides. The constable who attended the scene was unable to keep up with the magistrate's horse and prevent him from being assaulted. The locals, equipped with hatchets and hammers, made arrangements to saw up the masts and for carts to carry away their loot. Unfortunately, the crew of sixteen perished, except for the carpenter. The wreck was one of three during the particular week, with one vessel shedding its load of oranges and lemons, no doubt to the delight of local children.

The Ferryside Lifeboat service opened in 1835 and has since saved many lives. The crew of the *Craigwhinnie* of Liverpool, which went down in 1899, owed their lives to the lifeboat service. The wreck is still visible at low tide.

4

TOWN AND COUNTRY

Carmarthenshire is primarily a rural county. Its population density at eighty-one persons per sq.km compares to an all-Wales average of 152 persons per sq.km. The most industrialised and populated parts of the county are in the south and south-east.

TOWNS

Llanelli is by far the largest town (*c.* 26,000), followed by Carmarthen (*c.*15,000), Ammanford (*c.* 5,500) and Kidwelly (*c.* 3,700). The South Wales Coalfield extends into Carmarthenshire, which in its heyday centred on Llanelli, Ammanford and the Upper Gwendraeth Valley. Penygroes, Tumble, Pontyberem and Trimsaran developed as industrial villages. The area is dotted with the relics of its industrial past including sealed-up mineshafts, tunnels, quarries, disused railway lines, miners' cottages and other buildings. The docks at Llanelli and Burry Port linked the county to the wider world.

Carmarthen

Originally Carmarthen was called Moridunum, a name based on the old Celtic Brythonic terms *mori* (sea) and *dunon* (fort). The word survives in modern Welsh as *dinas* (city). Moridunum was the Roman regional headquarters, established to control the crossing point of the River Tywi. The fort was located between Parade Road and the Castle, while a civil settlement developed east of the fort. The Romans occupied the town until the fifth century, when troops were redeployed in mainland Europe.

In 1109, Henry I ordered the building of a castle on the ridge above the River Tywi. A new town developed around the castle, which meant that Carmarthen was effectively two fortified settlements. Traditionally, Carmarthen was a market town with cattle markets and horse fairs, while Fair Lane was once the site of an old hiring fair. Throughout the Middle Ages there were strong commercial rivalries between the old and new towns which were not settled until the Tudor years, when these were combined to form the borough of Carmarthen. The wealth of the town hinged on the river and the quayside is dominated by the Tywi Works, the oldest surviving business in the town, which started trading in 1795. The awkwardly shaped building was originally a coal depot and then an ironmonger's shop. The present building was completed in 1909 and flatteringly described by the *Carmarthen Journal* as 'the eighth wonder of the world'.

The modern history of Carmarthen has seen the decline of its iron industry, expansion in education, tourism and retail, and the redevelopment of the centre. In 1998 the Greyfriars Centre opened, the old market was incorporated into St Catherine's Walk Shopping Centre in 2010 and modest retail parks were established at Pensarn and off the Llangunnor roundabout. Road connections improved when the A48 was made a dual carriageway, linked to the M4, and the eastern bypass was built in 1999. The Pont King Morgan footbridge, which opened in 2006 and links the railway station to the town, was named after the King Morgan family, who served as chemists in Carmarthen for most of the twentieth century. In 1869 James Brigstocke was the first qualified chemist in the town and operated from 'The Pharmacy' (No. 25 King Street), selling everything from cough medicine to veterinary ointments. D. King Morgan subsequently acquired his business in the early twentieth century. The County Museum includes a large collection of the shop's apothecary jars. Carmarthen remains the headquarters for the county council, Dyfed–Powys Police, the Inland Revenue and the Department for Environment, Food and Rural Affairs (DEFRA).

Llanelli

Before the development of the iron, tin and coal industries, Llanelly was a small fishing village. In 1566, there were only twelve houses. It is now the largest town in the county, with a town population of around 26,000.

Llanelly House is the town's premier historic attraction, regarded as one of the finest restored Georgian houses in Wales. It was runner-up in the BBC *Restoration* series aired in 2003. It took ten years to restore the house, which opened in 2014. When it was first built in 1714 (the date can be seen on the cast-iron down-pipe in the front of the house), it had large gardens, upon which the main streets of the town were subsequently built. One of the house's mysteries is a sandstone heart found embedded in a blocked-up doorway in the east wall. During the restoration, a large collection of clay tobacco pipes were found in concealed voids, some dating back to the sixteenth century. Also on show is part of an impressive dinner service from China, commissioned by Sir Thomas Stepney.

Llanelli's transformation from small village to one of the leading industrial centres in Wales began with the ironmaster Alexander Raby, who opened an ironworks at Furnace in 1795. Raby's railway, which connected Cross Hands to Llanelly Dock, was the first operational mineral railway in the world under Act of Parliament. It was not long before four furnaces operated in the town, making cannons marked with their owner's initials 'A.R.' Pentrepoeth – literally meaning 'hot village' – is a reminder of the times.

In 1795, the town's population was around 500. By 1801, it had reached 2,000. But visitors were not impressed, dismissing it as 'a small, irregular and dirty town' and 'a miserable dirty place filled with miners and sailors'. Industrialisation disfigured the local landscape. However, economically, the town was prospering. In 1815 a guide described it as 'one of the most thriving places in South Wales'. By 1876 a travel guide confidently predicted that Llanelli was to become one of the most important commercial ports in Wales. It accepted, however, that there was little to attract or detain the tourist.

After the Second World War, there were major clearances of slums, derelict tinworks and factories. By 1957, when a local librarian filmed the demolishing programme, there were only three out of eighteen tinplate works remaining in the area. The town suffered economically in 1979, with the closure – after 130 years – of the Glanmorfa Foundry, followed by the Duport Steelworks. More than 1,000 people lost their jobs, despite appeals and even prayers. Unemployment in the town reached 19 per cent.

During the 1980s and '90s, council leaders sought to reinvent Llanelli as a seaside town. In 1987, the Duport Steelworks was demolished and the area landscaped. The walls of the Sandpiper restaurant, built in 1996, are lined with bricks from the old brickworks and display old photographs of the industrialised area. The development of the 2,000-acre Millennium coastal park during the 1990s has undoubtedly improved the environment. North Dock has been transformed for water sports, alongside a top golf course at Machynys, a cycle path connecting Llanelli to Burry Port and a visitors' centre. The redevelopment of the town focused on the new St Elli shopping centre, which opened in 1999. Trostre Retail Park has expanded considerably since it opened in 1989, picking up custom from supporters attending the 15,000-capacity Parc y Scarlets nearby. The stadium represents the emotional hub of the county. Llanelli town centre has benefited from further recent investment including the development of East Gate, a £26 million shopping centre, a £15 million state-of-the-art theatre (Ffwrnes) and the Selwyn Samuel Centre, a six-rink indoor bowling green.

In 2020/1, Carmarthenshire County Council announced major plans to redevelop the town centre and surroundings. These include a new Wellness Centre at Delta Lakes, but the plans were put on hold because of the Covid-19 pandemic.

Burry Port

The name of the village reflects its seafaring past. The harbour was built in the 1830s and was once busy exporting coal from the pits in the Gwendraeth Valley. In 2002 Carmarthenshire Council published the 700-page *Industrial and Maritime History of Llanelli and Burry Port, 1750 to 2000* (Craig et al., 2002) and the publication is an acknowledgement of the important contribution Burry Port made to the Industrial Revolution that made Britain 'the workshop of the world'. The book details the rise and fall of the region's coal, metal and maritime industries. There were also many subsidiary employments – the area was once alive with the noise of those making chains, ropes, anchors, pumps and sails for the ships, suppliers of food and clothes to meet the needs of sailors, and those busy breaking up old ships, trading scrap iron and repairing everything from compasses to masts.

Overlooking the Burry Estuary is Cilymaenllwyd ('seat of grey rock'), which has served as a residential care home since 1985. The original house, built in 1541, was replaced in the nineteenth century and passed into the hands of the Howard-Stepney family of Llanelly House, Carmarthenshire, in the 1900s. Margaret Stepney, known locally as Marged Fach (Small Margaret), was very fond of Dylan Thomas. She also liked a drink; Thomas described her as 'Marged gin woman'. On 22 January 1953 she committed suicide in London by taking an overdose of sleeping pills. Thomas found the news difficult to bear, not only because he had lost a close friend, but also because she left no will and had promised him to pay the expenses of maintaining the boathouse at Laugharne.

In 1932, Amelia Earhart became the first woman to fly the Atlantic, in an against-the-odds feat after her plane almost ran out of fuel. Four years earlier she had been a passenger on a flight from Nova Scotia, which crash-landed in Burry Port. Griff Bevan, who was a 14-year-old schoolboy at the time, recalled the event:

> I remember the plane landing as if it were yesterday. I was sitting at home having lunch. There was this droning noise and I knew it must have been a plane. I had heard about planes, of course, but I'd never seen one. I ran outside and saw it fly over the house. It had the name Friendship painted on the outside. We watched it go down and land in the estuary.

Since the tide was out, it was easy to row out and collect the crew from the seaplane. They thought that they had reached Ireland. The George Hotel in Burry Port has a 'Friendship Bar' to convey the story, including several paintings of Earhart. When Earhart returned to America, she was greeted with a ticker-tape parade in New York and a reception held by President Calvin Coolidge at the White House.

Ammanford

Metal statues of Twrch Trwyth, the wild boar and her piglets, greet visitors to Ammanford. They are reminders of the complex story about King Arthur chasing Twrch Trwyth (a wicked Irish king turned into a wild boar) and his followers across this part of the world. Arthur battles the creatures at Mynydd Amanw before pursuing Twrch Trwyth to the River Severn, where it is driven into the sea.

Technically speaking, the English road sign 'Welcome to Ammanford' is wrong – according to Huw Walters, a leading expert on Welsh place names, the 'Aman' should have one m rather than two (as is also the case with Amman, Brynamman, and Rhosamman). The only letters which double in Welsh are 'n' and 'r'. Amanford (with one 'm') is technically the correct form. The Welsh name, Rhydaman, was adopted a few years later.

Ammanford is the newest of Carmarthen's towns. It was originally called Beremfawr (highest rising ground) and then Cross Inn, named after one of several inns that stood at a crossroads in the centre of the village (what is now Ammanford Square). In 1851, less than 300 people lived at Cross Inn. The expansion of anthracite mining and tinplate production meant that the workforce increased substantially – by 1911, the population exceeded 6,000. Before 1831, when a bridge over the River Loughor was erected, travellers on their way to Carmarthen often used the shortest route along the Amman Valley. The inns provided the necessary refreshments although only the Old Cross Inn survives, refurbished in 2010.

The chapel and church communities had expressed concerns over the name of the village, especially given that the largest chapel in the village (i.e Cross Inn Chapel) bore the name of a public house. Locals also wanted to avoid confusion with another Cross Inn within the county. One vainglorious suggestion, put forward by the estate manager for the Dynevors, was to change the name to Dynevorville. However, despite the power of the gentry, the new name of Ammanford was adopted in 1880, leaving the chair of the deciding panel to quip that 'Cross Inn' had finally been 'crossed out'. The new name referred to a well-established ford of the River Amman located at what is now known as Betws Bridge.

The expansion of Ammanford was due to the coal and tinplate industries. By the 1880s, the latter employed around 1,200 workers. The population doubled from 3,058 (1901) to 6,074 (1911) and this led to the opening of new schools, miners' institutes and chapels, in which Welsh language culture particularly flourished.

In many cases, colliers held several jobs. Some continued to run smallholdings and work in the mines for part of the year. In the 1930s, the afternoon shift at Great Mountain Colliery, Tumble, was known as the 'Cardi' (i.e. Cardiganshire) shift, since many of the workers were small farmers who travelled in from Cardiganshire for the working week, leaving their family to tend the holding, and returned to their homes only at weekends. The 'boom' years lasted until the 1930s, when heavy industries went into decline.

Llandeilo

The town is named after the sixth-century St Teilo, who lived at the same time as Saint David. Legend has it that Teilo was so popular that three clergymen wanted the kudos of burying him when he died. To avoid confrontation, they agreed to pray for resolution. When they rose, they were shocked to find three corpses! These were removed to three locations: Llandaff Cathedral, at his birthplace in Penally, near Tenby and in Llandeilo (his chief church). A cult developed around St Teilo that is reflected in the twenty-three churches named after him in Wales, as well as one in Brittany. The church, built in 1850, dominates the town.

The town's greatest treasure is the eighth-century Llandeilo Fawr Gospels, written in Latin. But it also includes marginal notes in Welsh noting the community's possessions, making this the earliest surviving examples of written Welsh. According to folklore, a local man presented the book to the church, having bought it 'for the price of a good horse'. The book has different names, reflecting competing claims, including the Lichfield Gospels, the Chad Gospels, the Book of Chad, the Gospels of St Chad and St Teilo Gospels. By the eleventh century, the book found itself at Litchfield Cathedral, where it has remained. The bishops of Lichfield still swear allegiance to the Crown on the Lichfield (Llandeilo Fawr) Gospels. The book has recently been digitised and selected pages can be viewed at https://lichfield.as.uky.edu.

Travel writers have often criticised the appearance of Llandeilo. Mrs Morgan of Ely wrote of the town in 1791:

> I thought the town of Llandovery a miserable one but this of Llandeilo much worse. I never saw a place which had a more deplorable appearance. The streets, if so they may be called, are narrow and dirty and half-paved with stones, the sharp ends upwards. The houses are built from a kind of stone; but it is of so crumbling [a] nature that they appear to be falling into a decay. The inhabitants are very decent in their manners and in their outward semblance; they do not seem fit tenants for such wretched dwellings.

King George IV's visit to the town in 1822 is commemorated in the street names of King Street, George Street and George Hill. Rhosmaen Street was constructed as the main thoroughfare in the 1840s, splitting the huge churchyard in two, while the railway reached the town in 1856. When the first stone bridge was built in 1848, it was regarded as one of the 'Wonders of Wales'. One young lady returning from church boldly walked across the parapet, only to lose her balance and fall into the river – fortunately, she was saved when her skirt opened like a parachute to ease her landing.

The most detailed descriptions of everyday life in the town can be found in the writings of the local cabinet-maker, Thomas Jenkins. He was born at Tycroes and kept a diary from 1826 to 1871, shortly before he died at the age of 58. Jenkins describes buildings, people, fairs, food, streets and funerals.

Jenkins was an amazing character. His day job was making cabinets and coffins. But his interests covered astronomy, engineering, science, technology and nature. He walked to Pembroke Dock to see the warships and dockyard, collected fossils, observed the skies, built boats, made violins, created wax figures to display at the Great Exhibition in 1851, inspected breweries in Birmingham and acted as a census enumerator. He regularly walked to Carmarthen each week and on one occasion carried his daughter on his back to Llanelli, before he invented a 'homomotive carriage with three wheels' – a kind of heavy iron tricycle for passengers.

The fortunes of Llandeilo were tied closely to the Dinefwr family, the major landowners in the area. In 1883 they owned 7,208 acres throughout the county (not to mention lands in Glamorgan and English counties), which brought them an income from rents of £12,562 a year (worth around £600,000 today). Their main residence was Dynevor Park, in an estate that included the castle and mock-gothic Newton House. Parts of the house, such as the staircase, date to the 1660s. The National Trust has carried out extensive restoration work over recent years. The parkland, designed by Capability Brown, is packed with history and includes an Iron Age hill fort, two Roman forts and two medieval townships, but very little of it is visible.

Llangyndeyrn

The village is named after Cyndeyrn, who is believed to be a descendant of Cunedda, the fifth-century Welsh ruler who fought against Irish invasion. In more recent times, the villagers have had another battle on their hands. In 1960, they successfully prevented the village from being flooded to build a reservoir to supply water for the city of Swansea. Instead, the reservoir was built at Llyn Brianne, where there was no village to lose. On the fiftieth anniversary, in 2013, villagers cycled home from Llyn Tryweryn near Bala in North Wales, where the Capel Celyn campaign against flooding had failed.

Llandovery

Four rivers make their way through the market town of Llandovery, reflected in its Welsh name Llanymddyfri, which means 'the church amidst the waters' (from *llan*, 'church enclosure', and *ymlith-y-dyfroed*, 'amidst the waters'). The waters in question are the rivers Tywi, Bran, Y Bawddwr and Gwydderig.

Over the centuries, Llandovery has not been popular with the tourists. John Leland described it in the 1530s as a poor market town of one street, containing badly built thatched houses. Subsequent travel writers considered it to be 'the dirtiest town' and 'the most forbidding' in Wales. However, George Borrow offered a more positive view in 1854 when he wrote: 'Llandovery is a small but beautiful town situated among fertile meadows.'

The town is most noted for its public school, Llandovery College, founded by the surgeon Thomas Phillips in 1848. The early curriculum included Welsh, English, Latin, Greek, Hebrew, Arithmetic, Algebra, Mathematics, History and Geography. Girls were first admitted in the late 1960s. The scholastic tradition is also apparent in the publications that rolled off the town's nineteenth-century printing press, set up by William Rees. These included Charlotte Guest's translation of the *Mabinogion*, the famous collection of Welsh folktales.

Llandovery was a major drovers' centre. In 1799 a drover called David Jones opened the Black Ox Bank. He was an opportunist who saw the appeal of providing fellow drovers with 'notes of promise' rather than bags of gold sovereigns. He printed his own bank notes and the business was eventually taken over by Lloyds Bank in 1909.

Newcastle Emlyn

The richly painted shop fronts of Newcastle Emlyn add a splash of colour to the average high street. Only an archway and a few stones remain of the medieval 'new' castle that was built on the River Teifi. It was first mentioned in 1215 and suffered destruction at various times before it was blown up in the Civil Wars. The earlier castle was Cilgerran in Emlyn Is, which finally fell to the English in 1288. Information panels at the Cawdor market hall, a Grade II listed building, usefully explain the local heritage.

Pencader

People have been living in Pencader for at least 3,000 years, based on analysis of Bronze Age findings. Iron Age hill forts were built in the area and the Romans are likely to have passed through along the Sarn Helen.

The remains of Pencader Castle date back to the twelfth century; we know that King Henry II visited the castle in 1163 to receive homage from Lord Rhys of Deheubarth. Gerald of Wales tells the story of the Old Man of Pencader, who joined the king's forces against his own people 'because of their evil way of life'. The king asked the man whether the Welsh would resist and who would win. In 1952 Plaid Cymru, the Welsh nationalist party, etched his reply on slate and erected it as a memorial in the village:

> My Lord king, this nation may
> now be harassed, weakened and
> decimated by your soldiery, as it has
> so often been by others in former
> times; but it will never be totally
> destroyed by the wrath of man,
> unless at the same time it is punished
> by the wrath of God. Whatever else
> may come to pass, I do not think
> that on the Day of Direst Judgement
> any race other than the Welsh, or
> any other language, will give answer
> to the Supreme Judge of all for this
> small corner of the earth.

St Clears

We know hardly anything about the origins of St Clears. We know that the Normans built a motte and bailey castle here and that Gerald of Wales passed through the area in the twelfth century as part of his official tour of the country. He mentions, but does not explain, the murder of a young Welshman by twelve archers from the castle at St Clears. They were 'signed with the cross' as a punishment for the crime, which suggests that they may have joined to fight in the Crusades. In the 1840s, St Clears became embroiled in the Rebecca riots, which are commemorated by a modern sculptured gate.

An arts and crafts gallery, known as The Gate, showcases the work of local artists (www.the-gate.org). St Clears was home to Stanley Phillips, a local photographer, who documented life in the town during the early twentieth century. His studio was in the building now occupied by Philip Hughes the Butcher. Phillips took photographs of many villages around Carmarthenshire. He also photographed Sir Malcolm Campbell and Parry Thomas, both of whom tried to break the world land speed records at nearby Pendine Sands.

Whitland

The name 'Whitland' (Hendy-gwyn) may have come from the White House (Ty Gwyn) where Hywel Dda's parliament met; others think that it is associated with the white cloaks worn by the monks of the medieval Cistercian abbey founded in the twelfth century by Bernard, the bishop of St Davids. The Cistercians followed a severe lifestyle. They ate once a day, a meal of coarse bread, vegetables, herbs and beans. They had fish, eggs and other delicacies only on special anniversaries. Henry VIII eventually dissolved the abbey in 1539, but the ruins are still visible.

Kidwelly

Nennius, a ninth-century monk, first mentioned the name of Kidwelly (Cetgueli) which probably derives from a combination of the two words '*cyd*' (joint) and '*gweli*' (bed) which meant the joining of two rivers, namely the Gwendraeth Fawr and Fach. As a settlement, Kidwelly owes its origin to the castle established by the Normans in the 1100s, built on the bank of the River Gwendraeth to control trade. Princess Gwenllian led local opposition to the Norman invasion, culminating in her defeat in 1136. The scene of the battle is remembered in the name of the field, Maes Gwenllian, which lies about a mile north of the castle.

The castle has proved an inspiration for artists working for Sculpture Cymru, who began exhibiting their work in the castle in 2010. The artists have designed pieces that reflect the architecture, history and geography of the castle. Among the former exhibits were a dog lurking in the gateway and an owl perched high, scanning its domain. Current works of art include the Throne, which took its inspiration from the four massive towers of the inner ward, and a magnificent life-size stag.

Kidwelly played a key part in the Industrial Revolution. The town had a large brickworks and tinworks. Kidwelly Industrial Museum is on the site of the second oldest recorded tinplate works in the UK. It is a unique museum, dedicated to the interpretation of the tinplate industry.

Ferryside

The village is named after the ferry service, which operated for nearly 1,000 years. In 1170, the Knights Hospitaller at Slebech were awarded the right of running a ferry (the lifeboat at Ferryside still has the link). In 1188, Gerald of Wales used the ferry during his journey through Wales. It was an important crossing point for pilgrims making their way to the cathedral at St Davids. The last ferry across the Tywi was launched in 1948. The modern fisherman's statue is a reminder of the village's heritage.

Llanarthney

One of the most unusual sights in Carmarthenshire is Paxton's Tower, a folly erected by Sir William Paxton of Middleton Hall as a tribute to Lord Nelson. There are other theories. One story suggests that Paxton built it to console himself after he failed to gain council approval to build a bridge over the Tywi. Another claims it followed Paxton's narrow defeat at a parliamentary election in 1802, despite spending a fortune (around £500,000 by today's standards) on courting potential voters – this included 8,879 bottles of port and more than 11,000 breakfasts. A female traveller in 1860 complained that Paxton's Tower did not offer ice cream and pastries, unlike Edinburgh, but at least a free night's lodging to anyone at a loss. The tower is now something of a roofless shell.

GRADE I LISTED BUILDINGS

Grade I listed buildings are classified as of 'exceptional interest', being of special architectural, historical, or cultural significance. This means that strict limitations are imposed on the modifications allowed to a building's structure or fittings. Carmarthenshire's Grade I buildings are as follows:

- St Margaret's church, Marloes.
- Llansteffan Castle, LLansteffan.
- St Peter's church, Carmarthen.
- Carmarthen Castle.
- Outer Gatehouse, Laugharne Castle.
- Newcastle Emlyn Castle.
- St Michael's church, Cilycwm.
- Plas Taliaris, Manordeilo and Salem.
- Dryslwyn Castle, LLangathen.
- St Michael's church, Myddfai.
- Dolauhirion Bridge, Cilycwm.
- St Mary's church, Llandovery.
- Dinefwr Castle, Llandeilo.
- Kidwelly Castle.
- St Mary's church, Kidwelly.
- Llanelly House, Llanelli.
- Nos 20, 22 and 24 Vaughan Street, Llanelli (former rear wing of Llanelly House).
- Carreg Cennen Castle, Dyffryn Cenne.

Kidwelly Castle

WHAT'S IN A NAME?

The importance of names was well illustrated by Ann Beale, a writer who lived in Llandeilo in the mid-nineteenth century.

Two or three families of the same name live next door to each other, one selling haberdashery, another meat and a third gingerbread. Half-a-dozen Joneses may dwell in the same house and as many Evanses may dine at the same table, yet all be totally unconnected with each other. Without names to the streets, therefore, the postmaster would find considerable difficulty in knowing to which of the hundred or so Joneses, Jenkinses or Evanses he must send the different letters and a stranger in discovering the particular Mr, Mrs or Miss Rees he came to visit.

Many of the county's villages grew up around a crossroads. Examples include:

- Cross Hands – probably derived from the custom of handing over custody of prisoners, with their hands bound together, en route to Swansea prison.
- Five Roads – literally five roads, each leading off the centre of the village.
- Tycroes – derived from the cottage or house (*Ty*) that once stood at the village square.

Carmarthen (Caerfyrddin)

People still debate the origin of the Welsh name Caerfyrddin (Carmarthen), a corruption of the Latin Moridunum, or a name showing the birthplace of the wild magician Myrddin (Merlin). To make things even more complicated, the Roman writer Antonius actually called the town Muridunum, 'the walled city', whereas Ptolemy referred to it as Maridunum, with 'a' in the first syllable ('the fort by the sea'). In fact, most scholars think that the most accurate version is Moridunum (without the 'u' or 'a'!).

Over time the town acquired the prefix *caer* (which also meant 'fort') and contracted to *myrddin*, reflecting the town's association with Myrddin Emrys, or Merlin, the legendary wizard companion of King Arthur. The place name in Welsh duly became Caerfyrddin (Merlin's City), anglicised as Carmarthen.

Lammas Street (Carmarthen)

This is named after 'Loaf-mass' Day, i.e. 1 August, which was a harvest festival when loaves of bread made from the first ripe corn were consecrated.

Goose Lane (Carmarthen)

As well as cattle, geese were also taken on long journeys to English markets. The Welsh name for St Catherine Street in Carmarthen is actually Heol y Gwyddau (Goose Street). The flocks were prepared for the long journey to the markets in the Midlands and the eastern counties by first walking over pitch or tar and then over fine sand. When the feet became dry and hard they were then ready to be driven without injury on their long journeys. Sheep, pig and goose sculptures can be seen on Carmarthen's former market ground, which is now a shopping complex.

Maerdy, near Ammanford

Maerdy is a small village near Ammanford. It is an early medieval Welsh word meaning 'slave's house' (*maer,* slave; *dy,* house). In medieval times, slaves could not leave the farms without the landowners' permission; if the land was sold, the slave became the property of the new owner. Later, *maerdy* changed its meaning to 'house of the mayor' because the mayor was the official responsible for slave markets. In Gorseinon, there is a pub called The Mardy.

Bynea, near Llanelli

The Welsh name for this small village near Llanelli is Y Bynie and one suggestion is that this derives from a corruption of the phrase '*heb un iau*', meaning 'without a yoke'. This refers to the common practice of allowing oxen untethered in the River Loughor.

Caio

The full parish title of this village is Cynwyl Caio, which means 'advanced guards of Caius'. This is a reminder of the importance the Romans attached to protecting the nearby Dolaucothi gold mines.

Caius may have been in charge of the troop detachment. Many red Roman bricks have been ploughed up in the area.

Machynis (Llanelli)

Machynis is a corruption of a term meaning 'Monk's island'. In medieval times, the area was an island upon which St Piero established a monastery and it remained as such until 1536, when Henry VIII broke up the religious houses. As late as the eighteenth century, maps and plans show Machynis was still an island.

Llanybydder

The origins of the village name are uncertain but literally speaking, *llan* refers to the area around a church and *y byddder* means 'of the deaf.' In the thirteenth century, Gwenllian of Blaen Tren had founded a female religious order in the vicinity and the vow of silence taken by the nuns could have caused people to think that they were deaf.

Login

This tiny hamlet set up high in the Taf Valley was originally based around a mill. The name probably derives from the Welsh word *halogyn*, meaning 'a dirty stream'.

Drover's Arms, The Drovers, Drover's Halt, Drover's Rest, Jolly Drover, Black Ox

Prior to the development of the iron and coal industries, Wales' chief produce lay in the breeding of stock. In particular, large numbers of cattle were annually driven along famous routes to major English fairs, where farmers bought them to be fattened either in yards and buildings in autumn and winter, or on good pastures during summer. There are clues to Carmarthenshire's contribution in pub and place names. In the village of Cilycwm, above ground, there is a cobbled, man-made watercourse, running along one side of the roadway. This provided water for the cattle collected on other side of the road during fair days.

Before setting off on their long journey over rough trackways, the cattle were assembled and shod by skilled blacksmiths. The herds of up to 150 beasts were driven an average of 12–15 miles each day while the drovers would rest up after ten hours of walking at inns such as Traveller's Rest, Half Way, Tafarn Jem and the Ram Inn (Cwmann). The Tafarn Jem was originally called the Mountain Cottage Inn but soon changed its name to acknowledge the services of the landlady, Jemima, who was very hospitable to walkers. South of the village of Caio are earthwork remains of drovers' enclosures. At the turn of the eighteenth century, the drovers were usually paid 3s daily and a bonus of 6s, given after the cattle were sold at fairs such as Smithfield or Barnet.

Links with markets in London are reflected in place names such as Piccadilly Square (Llanboidy); Charing Cross (Llandeilo); Llundain and Llundain Fach (Llanelly and Caio); Temple Bar (numerous); Rhiw Sais; Pont i'r Sais (Conwil Elfed); and Smithfield (Llanybyther).

Turks
No one knows for certain why Llanelli people are called 'Turks'. Some say it began when a Turkish ship tried to dock at Swansea but permission was refused and the ship was sent on to Llanelli. Others say that during the First World War, Llanelli men recruited to the Fourth Welsh Regiment fought in Palestine and defeated the Turks.

5

THE PEOPLE OF CARMARTHENSHIRE

Carmarthenshire has had its darker side and fair share of shady characters, like all counties. But it has also had its heroes whose achievements have been widely admired and left their mark on the local and sometimes national stage.

CARMARTHENSHIRE GREATS

Merlin (possibly fifth century AD)
Visitors to Carmarthen are greeted by an impressive wooden sculpture on Merlin's walk, to commemorate arguably the county's

most celebrated figure. There is plenty of mystery surrounding Merlin, or Myrddin Emrys, as befitting a wizard. The Merlin we know today owes much to the writings of a twelfth-century monk and traveller, Geoffrey of Monmouth. His book, *History of the Kings of Britain*, became a bestseller and was soon translated into French. It spurred many legends about Merlinus, who became a central figure in European literature. According to Geoffrey, Merlin was born to a virgin nun in Carmarthen and lived in a deep cave in what became known as Merlin's Hill, where he lives on.

Geoffrey of Monmouth presents Merlin as a boy magician at the court of Vortigern, King of the Britons. Later, as an adult wizard, Merlin changes the appearance of Uther Pendragon (the King of Camelot) so that he can sleep with the wife of the Duke of Cornwall. Out of this magic, the future King Arthur is conceived. Merlin then served as Arthur's adviser, prophet and magician.

Merlin is hard to pin down – his very name means 'myriad'. Michael Dames, who has written one of the best books on the subject, sees Merlin as a Welsh gift to humanity. But he admits that Merlin has many sides. He tamed two dragons for King Vortigern at Dinas Emrys (near modern Beddgelert in Snowdonia), supposedly overlooked the building of Stonehenge, and took the ancient treasures of Britain to the sacred island of Bardsey. It has to be said that there are also less flattering stories of Merlin as a shape-shifting demon who ends up imprisoned in a rock for all eternity.

Merlin's Oak once stood on the corner of Oak Lane and Priory Street in Carmarthen. Local legend has it that Merlin placed the following protective curse on the tree:

> When Merlin's Oak shall tumble down,
> Then shall fall Carmarthen Town.

A schoolmaster probably planted the tree in 1659 to celebrate the return of King Charles II to the English throne. A local man poisoned the tree in the early nineteenth century, to stop people from meeting under it. In 1951, a branch was broken off from the tree and can be seen in the County Museum. In 1978, the last

Charles II

fragment of the tree was relocated to Saint Peter's Civic Hall in Nott Square, Carmarthen.

Hywel Dda (c. AD 890–c. AD 950)

Hywel Dda (the Good) founded a kingdom that covered roughly the present three south-west counties and Gower, although his influence extended further afield. He was the first and only king in Wales to mint his own coins but he is most famous for creating Wales' first legal system. He is held as a true Welsh hero, commemorated in the names of a health board, school, restaurants and hotels.

William Williams (1717–91)

Regarded by some as the greatest Welsh poet, Williams was also a famous preacher and hymn writer, composing nearly 1,000 hymns. They were popular because they were simple, easily remembered and had a great tune – on one occasion, hundreds of people gathered to sing a collection of Williams' hymns for three consecutive days, much like a modern pop festival.

Much of the passion associated with the Welsh character is attributed to Williams. The opening verse of his most famous work conjures up a unique atmosphere when sung at the Millennium Stadium to stir on the national side:

> Guide me, O thou great Jehovah,
> pilgrim through this barren land;
> I am weak, but thou art mighty,
> hold me with thy powerful hand:
> bread of heaven! bread of heaven!
> feed me now and evermore ...

Griffith Jones (1683–1761)

Griffith Jones was the individual most responsible for making the majority of Welsh speakers literate for the first time in history. Born in Penboyr, Jones founded the Circulating Schools movement that was a major contribution to educating the Welsh and improving literacy levels. He was ordained as a priest and became rector of Llandeilo Abercywyn in 1711. His marriage to

William Williams

Margaret, sister of Sir John Phillips of Picton Castle, meant that he received much financial support. Jones realised that Welsh speakers would benefit from receiving an education in their home language, whereas the existing schools of the day taught through the medium of English. In 1731 he began his ambitious scheme and supported teachers by publishing over thirty books, mostly to do with religious teaching. It is estimated that, by the time of his death, around 200,000 people – one in two of the country's population – had attended one of his schools and achieved some degree of literacy. This figure included adults as well as children. Jones also opened a training academy for teachers at Llanddowror, although they were paid a miserable £3–£4 per annum (around £250–£350 by today's standards). News of his success reached Catherine the Great, Empress of Russia, who sent an ambassador to Wales to see what she could learn in her desire to educate the Russian people.

Bridget Bevan (1698–1779)

Madam Bevan, as she was called, was one of the most important women in Welsh history. She was a major patron of education. She was from a wealthy gentry family, daughter of John Vaughan of Derllys Court. A deeply religious woman, she became the main supporter of Griffith Jones' Circulating Schools, which did so much to improve reading skills through the use of the Bible and other religious texts. Madam Bevan led the movement after his death. In her will, she left £10,000 (around £630,000 today) to the work but the legacy was challenged and not released until 1809, by which time the movement had lost its impetus. The last schools closed in 1854. The only known portrait of Madam Bevan can be seen at the County Museum.

Twm Sion Cati (Thomas Jones, 1530–1609)

Often styled 'the Welsh Robin Hood', Twm Sion Cati is associated with Llandovery. In fact, he was a nobleman, scholar and respected poet. His alter ego – highwayman, trickster and womaniser – has been played out in films, stories and cartoons. In one story he entered an ironmonger's shop and held up a large pot against the light, declaring that it had a hole in it. The shopkeeper protested and so Twm pushed the pot over his head. 'Now, my friend, I presume you can see that the pot has a hole in it, because how else could you have got your head inside?' cried Tom, as he grabbed what he could on his way out. Twm's cave hideout can be visited as part of a RSPB reserve at Rhandirmwyn.

Thomas Charles (1755–1814)
He was born in Llanfihangel Abercowin and attended Llanddowror village school, Carmarthen Academy and then Jesus College, Oxford. He fell in love with Sally Jones, the daughter of a Bala shopkeeper, who refused to leave the area. So Charles was forever associated with Bala, where he joined the Methodists and became a leading figure in the Sunday school movement in Wales. He trained groups of travelling teachers, who taught Bible reading for six or nine months at a time in each locality He published teaching materials such as a Welsh spelling book and biblical commentary.

James Griffiths (1890–1975)
Griffiths was born and raised in the Welsh-speaking community of Betws, near Ammanford. His father was the local blacksmith. Like many children of the age, Griffiths left school at the age of 13 to work down the local colliery, where in time he became lodge secretary. He was a strong activist for the Labour Party and, by 1934, became president of the very powerful Miners' Federation of South Wales – The Fed. Two years later he was elected MP for Llanelli and served until 1970. He won eight elections and always secured at least 65 per cent of the vote. He became the first Secretary of State for Wales. While in government, he was instrumental in building the welfare state alongside another outstanding Welsh politician, Aneurin Bevan. When Griffiths died, the prime minister (James Callaghan) described him as 'one of the greatest sons of Wales'.

Dorothy Squires (1915–98)
Born in a showman's caravan at Bridge Shop Field, in Pontyberem, Squires became one of the most popular singers of the 1940s. Her 'rags-to-riches' career spanned six decades and took her from Llanelli Ritz to Hollywood. Among her friends and admirers

were Frankie Howerd, Petula Clarke, Diana Dors and Elvis Presley. She married the actor Roger Moore in 1953 but she never recovered from their divorce in 1969. She died from cancer in poverty in 1998. The late Sir Roger Moore agreed to pay for a blue plaque to commemorate his ex-wife's life, which was erected at the former family home in Dafen.

Rachel Roberts (1927–80)

Born in Llanelli and raised within a strong Baptist family (against which she rebelled), Roberts studied at the University of Wales and the Royal Academy of Dramatic Art. She made her film debut in 1953 in *Valley of Song*, a comedy set in Wales, and went on to star in several acclaimed films. Her second marriage was to Rex Harrison but this ended, like her first, in divorce. Sadly, she suffered depression and became an alcoholic, before finally committing suicide.

Dylan Thomas (1914–53)

Although born in a small house in Swansea, Thomas will always be strongly associated with Carmarthenshire. His grandparents lived in what is now a restaurant and pub in Johnstown known as 'Under Milk Wood', while his family originated from Brechfa. But it is Laugharne that has the greatest attachment and inspired his writing. He said that when he arrived here by bus, he simply forgot to get back on again. Laugharne folk claim that the village of Llareggub ('Bugger all' backwards), the subject of Dylan's radio play, *Under Milk Wood*, is based on their town. Thomas first arrived at the Boat House in 1949, where he lived until his premature death in 1953. He rented the property from his benefactor, Margaret Taylor (the wife of the famous historian A.J.P. Taylor). He penned six poems from Laugharne, beginning with 'Over Sir John's Hill'. He described the Boat House as his 'sea-shaken house on a breakneck of rocks'.

Dylan's favourite pub, the Edwinsford Arms, is now a restaurant, 'Yr Hen Dafarn'. Dylan noted its 'sabbath-dark bar with a stag's head over the Gents'. The best example of Dylan Thomas' love of Llansteffan can be gleaned from his comical story 'A Visit to Grandpa's'.

He had strong beer and I had lemonade, and he paid Mrs Edwinsford with a sovereign out of the tinkling bag; she inquired after his health, and he said that Llangadock was better for the tubes. We went to look at the churchyard and the sea, and sat in the wood called the Sticks, and stood on the concert platform in the middle of the wood where visitors sang on midsummer nights and, year by year, the innocent of the village was elected mayor. Grandpa paused at the churchyard and pointed over the iron gate at the angelic headstones and the poor wooden crosses. 'There's no sense in lying there,' he said.

The Sticks, probably named after mature fir trees felled in the 1950s, are the woods alongside the beach on the slopes below the castle. It is also the name of the former pub, restaurant and hotel close to the beach.

Thomas was in touch with many leading cultural figures of the day. His letters offer a fascinating insight into his character. In one letter to the writer Henry Treece, inviting him to stay at the Boat House, Thomas admitted that he was 'small, argumentative, good-tempered, lazy, fumbling, boozy as possible, lower middle class in attitude, a dirty tongue, a silly young man'.

Carwyn James (1929–83)

James was born in Cefneithin in the Gwendraeth Valley and became a Welsh teacher and lecturer. Although he played fly-half for Llanelli and was capped by Wales, he developed a reputation as a first-class coach, a reputation which was enhanced when his team beat the All Blacks in 1972. The year before, he also coached the British and Irish Lions during their successful tour of New Zealand, the only Lions side to win a series against the All Blacks.

Thomas Llew Jones (1915–2009)

T. Llew Jones, as he was known, was born in Pentrecwrt. He was a former head teacher who became an award-winning poet and arguably the most famous writer of Welsh-language children's books, especially historical novels. His career spanned fifty years. In 2012, a new Welsh-medium primary school in Brynhoffnant, near Llandysul, opened and was named after him. Jones wrote about historical characters such as the pirate Bartholomew Roberts and the highwayman Twm Sion Cati.

Terry Griffiths (1947–)

Griffiths was born in Llanelli and worked as a postman, miner and bus conductor. He turned professional snooker player in 1978 and won the world championship the following year. He was runner-up in 1988. He played his final season in 1997, completing 999 frames at snooker's headquarters, The Crucible.

Huw Edwards (1961–)

Although born in Bridgend, Edwards was raised in Llangennech from the age of 4 and later attended Llanelli Boys' Grammar School. His father was Hywel Teifi, a prominent Welsh historian. Edwards joined the BBC as a trainee journalist in 1984 and has established himself as the longest-serving news presenter on the BBC.

THE PHYSICIANS OF MYDDFAI

The Physicians of Myddfai served at the court of the Welsh prince, Rhys Gryg, who was killed attacking the Norman castle in Carmarthen in 1234. The Physicians are shrouded in mystery. Legend has it that their mother was a magical creature who passed on her knowledge about the medicinal value of plants before returning to her home, the lake of Llyn-y-Fan Fach. In recent years, the villagers of Myddfai have tried to exploit their traditions in an effort to reverse depopulation and decline. Backed by national lottery cash, they have launched a range of herbal remedies and other branded goods, designed to revive their village that was once renowned across medieval Europe for its healing abilities.

Excerpts from Some of the Physicians of Myddfai's Remedies
- **Comfrey**: the herb is useful to treat all wounds. Externally it is specific for chronic varicose ulcers. For gastric use it is often mixed with marshmallow and meadowsweet.

- **Cowslip**: used for the bite of a mad dog. Seek some cowslips, pound them, mix with milk and administer to the patient as their only drink for nine days, being first strained through a fine cloth.
- **Dandelion**: for the treatment of jaundice. Take dandelion, corn blue bottle and garden parsley. Pound them well, with a good strong ale, and keep the mixture carefully in a narrow mouthed water bottle.
- **Fennel**: useful for diseases of the eye. It is good for every kind of poison in a person's body.
- **Garlic**: for noise in the head, preventing hearing. Take a clove of garlic, dip it in honey and insert in the ear, covering it with some black wool. Let the patient sleep on the other side every night leaving the clove in the ear for seven or eight nights unchanged.

CARMARTHENSHIRE GRAVES

James Griffiths (1890–1975)
He was MP for Llanelli and a key figure behind the welfare state. He is buried in the cemetery behind Gellimanwydd chapel, Ammanford.

Dylan Thomas (1914–53)
The best-known Welsh writer is buried in St Martin's parish churchyard, Laugharne. A simple white cross marks his grave.

John Johnes (1800–76)
Johnes was a major landowner who was murdered by his butler, Henry Tremble, in 1876. Tremble then shot himself. The butler was buried at 11 p.m., but the villagers did not want him in the same graveyard as his victim and so Tremble's body was exhumed and removed to Llandulas in Breconshire. The parishioners of Llandulas objected to this and returned the coffin, dumping it outside Caio's churchyard. At Aber Bowlam they threw out the straw which covered the coffin and it remained there as a '*Bwgan*' (bogey) to scare children. In Caio churchyard, the Johnes family vault stands in contrast to the unmarked grave of Tremble.

Hugh Williams (1796–1874)

He was a radical lawyer who supported the Chartists and Rebecca rioters, and friend of President Abraham Lincoln. He is buried at St Ishmael's churchyard, Ferryside.

William Williams (1717–91)

Wales' finest hymn-writer is buried in Llanfair-ar-y-bryn churchyard, Llandovery.

Griffith Jones (1683–1761)

Wales' greatest eighteenth-century educator, Jones is buried in the chancel of Llanddowror church.

Sir Rhys ap Thomas (1449–1525)

The most influential Welshman in early Tudor times is buried in St Peter's church, Carmarthen.

Thomas Bowen (d. 1902)

Thomas Bowen was a carpenter and part-time undertaker, who allegedly died from rabies after a dog bite. The *Carmarthen Journal* reported that he became raving mad and terribly violent, requiring six men to hold him down. Money was raised to send him to the Pasteur Institute in Paris but he never recovered. Fred Pirkkis, chair of the National Canine Defence League, protested that there was no evidence that the dog was rabid and claimed that more than 1,200 people had died from Pasteur's 'terrible and most disgusting inoculations'. According to folklore, the local doctor finally smothered him to death between two mattresses. Bowen is buried beneath a huge yew tree in front of Hen Bethel Chapel in Garnant, overlooking the Amman Valley.

NOTES ON A FEW CARMARTHENSHIRE CENTENARIANS

History is not only about those in power. Here are a few humble people from around the county. They were ordinary in every respect other than the fact that they had reached the age of 100. These details are taken from the local newspapers.

William Rees, Garnant (1794–1898)

William Rees was born in Llandovery and known as the 'Pig killer' of the Lamb and Flag Inn, Garnant. He was one of fourteen children and spent fifty years working in the iron towns of Nantyglo and Merthyr. He recalled being press-ganged for the battle of Waterloo, but released due to his small stature. He died aged 104.

Elizabeth Evans, Abergwili (1781–1885)

Elizabeth Evans was born in Ffynon Felin. She walked the 10 miles to Carmarthen market every week for much her life, even after her 100th birthday. She had twenty grandchildren and half a dozen great-grandchildren at the time of her death. She died aged 103.

Rhys Thomas Lewis (1903–2012)

Rhys Lewis was born and raised in Llanelli. He claimed the title of the oldest Welshman when he died in 2012 at the age of 108. He left school to become a miner and then gained a scholarship to read history at Aberystwyth University. He qualified to become a lecturer in history in Wokingham, Berkshire. Two of his sisters, Doris and Megan, were 102 and 99 respectively when they died in 2011.

6

WELSH LANGUAGE AND CULTURE

Welsh is one of the oldest spoken languages in the world, but the rules for written Welsh were only standardised in the 1920s. Many Welsh place names have been 'anglicised', which means they have undergone slight variations in spelling to make them easier to pronounce for those more familiar with the English alphabet – for example, Llanymddyfri to Llandovery, Pont-iets to Pontyates. This is not a trivial matter. In 2013, the villagers of Varteg in Torfaen (Monmouthshire) were up in arms when Welsh language campaigners wanted to return the village to its Welsh name of Y Farteg (there is no letter 'V' in Welsh). As one local put it: 'Just imagine how embarrassing it will be to have the word fart in your village's name, never mind being followed by egg.' The idea of having standardised spellings of place names is quite a modern one and is linked to the introduction of Ordnance Survey maps.

According to the Office for National Statistics, in 2020 around 29 per cent of people aged three and over were able to speak Welsh in the whole of Wales. However, the most reliable data is tied to the national census taken every ten years. The findings from the 2021 Census are due to be released in 2022. Carmarthenshire remains a stronghold of Welsh language and culture, despite a steady decline in the number of Welsh speakers over the past hundred or so years. The Annual Population Survey of 2020 estimates around 92,000 Welsh speakers in Carmarthenshire, which is a marked increase from the 78,000 recorded in the 2011 census. There are variations within the county: the percentage of Welsh speakers in the old mining village of Pontyberem, for example, is about three times higher than Laugharne.

Increasingly over the past few decades, local and national government policies have championed the virtues of a bilingual society. Activities of groups such as Urdd Gobaith Cymru, the Young Farmer's Movement, Mentor Bro, Mudiad Ysgolion Meithrin and Merched y Wawr, along with local schools, have all energised the language among children and young people.

Education

In 1847, a landmark report appeared on the state of education in Wales. Its 1,252 pages made grim reading. Put simply, teachers were not well trained, there were not enough good-quality schools, resources were scarce, parents apathetic, children stupid and the Welsh language a hindrance to progress. The small schools run privately by single women or dames for a few pence each week were strongly condemned. The report, known as the 'Treachery of the Blue Books', angered many for its dismissive attitudes towards the Welsh language, Nonconformists and morality of the Welsh people.

Some 100 years after such a low point, a Welsh school opened in Llanelli, the first to be established by a local education authority in Wales. The impetus came largely from parents, as well as political pressures. The background was a clause within the Education Act (1944), which stated that parents should have a say in their children's education. A local school inspector, Matthew Williams, and others lobbied the Ministry of Education in London to support educating children 'in their mother tongue ... the language of our homes'. It took two years before approval was granted and the school opened in Zion's Chapel Vestry to thirty-four children, aged between 3 and 8.

Further Welsh-medium primary schools soon opened in the 1950s and '60s:

* Ysgol Brynsierfel, Llanelli – 1953
* Ysgol y Dderwen, Carmarthen – 1955
* Ysgol Teilo Sant, Llandeilo – 1958
* Ysgol Parc y Tywyn, Burry Port – 1965
* Ysgol Gymraeg Rhydaman, Ammanford – 1967
* Ysgol Gwenllian, Kidwelly – 1968

Inevitably this spurred a demand for Welsh medium secondary schools. Ysgol Gyfun y Strade opened in Llanelli in 1977, followed by Ysgol Gyfun Bro Myrddin, Carmarthen, in 1978 and Ysgol Gyfun Maes-yr-yrfa, Cefneithin, in 1983. Welsh then became a compulsory subject in the national curriculum in 1988. The local authority categorises schools according to their linguistic profile, along a continuum from Welsh medium to predominantly English medium, where Welsh is taught as a second language. Around two-thirds of primary schoolchildren in the county receive their education mainly in Welsh, while about a quarter do so in secondary schools. Pressures to close small rural schools on economic grounds complicate the position and there has been a move towards federated schools served by an itinerant head teacher. Adult classes for Welsh learners are also expanding, while the University of Wales Trinity Saint David has a proud bilingual tradition spanning three centuries (Welsh featured on the very first timetable in 1848).

The survival and development of the Welsh language is due largely to the efforts of a committed Welsh-speaking minority. Activists continue to fight against what they see as an anglicisation of everyday life, while other non-Welsh speakers sometimes consider themselves to be strangers in their own country. Nationalists have made significant progress over the past fifty years or so in securing greater status and recognition for the Welsh language, which has the potential to both unite and divide. In his book *In search of Welshness*, the writer Peter Daniels, a Welsh learner, describes taking his English-speaking wife to the Millennium National Eisteddfod in Llanelli. Upon putting on headphones to tune into the on-site translation service, the lady sitting next to him turned to her friend and, pointing at him, whispered '*Sais*' (Englishman). Daniels was offended at being branded a foreigner in his own land.

Plaid Cymru
In 1925 a new political party was formed in a guesthouse in Pwllheli, North Wales, called Plaid Genedlaethol Cymru (the National Party of Wales). Its leaders wanted an independent, self-governing Wales along the lines of the status enjoyed by the dominions of Canada, Australia and New Zealand. Members wanted to preserve what

they considered to be a unique Welsh way of life. Although growth was slow, by 1939 there were around 3,700 members affiliated to 139 branches, including Carmarthen and Llanelli. There was strong sympathy for three of the leaders when they were sentenced to nine months in prison for setting fire to a government 'bombing school' in 1937. Gwynfor Evans, brought up in an English-speaking home in Barry, took over as president in 1945 and achieved the most significant breakthrough for the party when he won the Carmarthen by-election in 1966, securing 16,177 votes (39 per cent). He held the position until 1981. Evans has been regarded as one of the most significant movers in promoting Welsh during the twentieth century. He counted gaining a parliamentary seat and the setting up of S4C, the Welsh television channel, as his greatest political achievements. (In 1980 he threatened to starve himself to death if a Welsh channel was not established.) In 2014, S4C announced that its new headquarters is to be located in Carmarthen, and in 2016 a plaque was erected outside Carmarthen's Guildhall to commemorate the 50th anniversary of Evans' victory as Plaid Cymru's first MP.

Eisteddfod

The eisteddfod (derived from the Welsh words *eistedd*, 'to sit', and *bod*, 'to be', hence 'to be sitting' or 'to be sitting together') is a Welsh festival of literature, music and performance. The first eisteddfod was held at Cardigan Castle in 1176 and Carmarthenshire held its first eisteddfod in 1451. The winning poet received a miniature silver chair, a silver crwth (stringed musical instrument) was awarded to the winning fiddler, a silver tongue to the best singer, and a small silver harp to the best harpist. The blind William Williams (1759–1828), known as 'Will Penmorfa', was particularly talented and was harpist to the Gwynne family at Tregib near Llandeilo.

Since 1952, the National Eisteddfod has been an exclusively Welsh-language festival for competitors. It is always held in the first full week of August, alternatively in North and South Wales. In 2014, the Eisteddfod was held in Llanelli. Local communities often hold their own eisteddfoddau to showcase varied talents in singing, dancing, poetry, drama, rural skills and crafts, such as folk dancing at Talog (Dawnswyr Talog).

CUSTOMS

The following customs were not exclusive to Carmarthenshire but common throughout rural Wales.

Plygain

The word Plygain derives from the Latin *pulli cantus*, that is to say 'the crowing of the cock at break of day'. Traditionally, this church service was held early in the morning, between 3 a.m. and 6 a.m. Sometimes people would gather at farmhouses and make treacle toffee (cyflaith) and decorate the house. Special candles were made to light up the procession to the church.

Mari Lwyd

The Mari Lwyd (Grey Mare or Holy Mary in Welsh) aimed to bring joy during the dark midwinter nights. The word *Mari* possibly originated from the English word for 'Mare' as the custom involved a horse's skull being carried on a pole covered by a long white sheet to conceal the bearer. During Christmas, the Mari was led from house to house to much merriment. The Mari chased after young women, seeking their affection.

Bundling

In the nineteenth century, 'bundling' or 'courting in bed' (*caru yn y gwely*) was very popular among young people. Typically, the man might throw pebbles at the girl's window and then use a ladder from the barn to enter and leave through the window. The practice was widely condemned by the authorities such as chapel and church ministers, not only for its immorality, but also for leading to unwanted pregnancy. An infamous government report on education in Wales in 1847 criticised the practice in older farmhouses where men and women were left alone together in the same bedroom, without a separating curtain.

Love spoons

In the eighteenth and nineteenth centuries, while seeking the affections of a young woman, it was the custom for a man to spend many hours carving a spoon with his own hands, in the hope that she would accept it. If she did, they would begin their courtship. Sometimes the girl's name was carved on the spoon along with a heart, ring or chain. A collection of love spoons from Carmarthenshire is on display at the County Museum.

Welsh love spoon

Bidding Letters

The Welsh custom of 'bidding' involved a wedding invitation sent by the couple to their friends and neighbours. It requested their attendance at the wedding, along with a contribution towards the purchase of articles they required to set up home. The prospective gifts were written down alongside the names and residences of the donors. In some cases, a bidder (*gwahoddwr*) would visit the homes of those to be invited, sometimes reciting hymns and singing rhymes, announcing the forthcoming wedding details. More often, the invitation took the form of a printed circular note. Typically, hundreds would be issued for a single marriage. The following example appeared in Carmarthen in 1872:

> It being our intention to enter the MATRIMONIAL STATE, on Friday, the 3rd day of November next, we are encouraged by our friends to make a BIDDING on the occasion, the same day; the Young Man at his Mother's house, called Cwmcelly fawr, in the parish of Llanfynydd, and the Young Woman at her Mother's house, called Troedyrhiw, in the parish of Llanfihangel-rhose-ycorn; at either of which places the favour of your good and most agreeable company is respectfully solicited; and whatever donation you may be pleased to confer on us then, will be thankfully received, and warmly acknowledged, and cheerfully repaid whenever called for a similar occasion.

By your most obedient servants,
Morgan Morgans
Anne Jones

The Sin Eater

The Sin Eater was someone who absolved the soul of a person by eating food at his or her funeral. A plateful of salt would be covered with a slice of bread and placed on the breast of the deceased. After certain charms were recited, the Sin Eater would then eat both bread and salt, washed down with beer. The act was said to transfer the sins from the deceased to the participant who was paid a meagre 6*d* for the trouble. He was then driven from the house and agreed never to return. So unruly were the inhabitants of the Amman Valley in the early 1800s, that someone composed the following verse as a testimony to their behaviour:

> All men in Cwmamman born,
> You are each one the Devil's spawn.
> Repent most quickly you must do
> Or he will take you, two by two.

GEORGIAN AND VICTORIAN VISITORS AND MIGRANTS

Since prehistoric times, people have visited West Wales for different reasons. Some have migrated in search of better lives; others have seized lands or visited as tourists. The Iron Age Celts came from mainland Europe. The Irish, Celtic brethren to many Welsh people, settled in West Wales soon after the Romans departed some 1,600 years ago. The Irish written language of Ogham can be seen inscribed on various ancient stones in the county alongside Latin. For example, the Clutorix Stone in Llandysilo parish church contains both languages and possibly refers to someone who learnt Latin at school.

In 1770, a Frenchman called Peter Du Buisson bought Glyndir estate on the outskirts of Llandybïe while travelling back from Ireland. He had been delayed by poor weather and decided to

Napoleon (Library of Congress, LC-USZ62-116232)

explore the area. He was so captivated by the building, originally a farmhouse, that he decided to buy it. The Du Buisson family were Huguenots fleeing persecution in France. By the nineteenth century the estate had its own brewery, carpenter's shop, mill, dovecote, slaughterhouse and knife factory. The production of knives caused rumours that the family were aiding the French in their fight against the English during the Napoleonic Wars. News of Napoleon's defeat reached Glyndir – ahead of anywhere else in the county – by carrier pigeon, given as a present to two of Du Buisson's cousins who were on holiday in 1814. Caroline Du Buisson acted swiftly on the news by setting out for London to buy government stocks (about to rise in value) before the news reached London from Waterloo. Her subsequent profits were used to build a girls' school locally, finance the building of Llandyfan church and refurbish the church at Llandybïe. In 1921, the Du Buisson estate was finally sold.

After the Great Potato Famine in Ireland during the 1840s, many Irish families escaped to Wales. They often lived in squalid conditions such as those in the one-bedroomed cottages (since demolished) of Carmarthen's poorest district of Dan-y-banc ('under the bank') near the river. The Irish-born population of Carmarthenshire rose from 163 in 1841 to 514 in 1851. However, this was well behind the additional 6,500 who poured into industrial Glamorgan in search of work, pushing Glamorgan's Irish population to nearly 10,000.

7

LANDSCAPE
AND WILDLIFE

Dylan Thomas was one of many writers, poets and artists
who have been inspired by the Carmarthenshire landscape.
For Thomas could see the beauty in the 'pebbly dab-filled shallow',
'the lamb white days', and the 'springful of larks in a rolling cloud'.

GARDEN OF WALES

Due to its rich, fertile lands, Carmarthenshire has been dubbed
'the garden of Wales' and has fed other parts of Britain for centuries.
Cattle herdsmen or drovers were once a familiar sight, making their
way through Llandovery to the markets in London and the Midlands.

The National Botanic Garden of Wales
The National Botanic Garden of Wales (NBGW) is set within
an estate dating back to the 1600s that was first owned by the
Middleton family. By the 1780s, the estate had passed into William
Paxton's hands for about £40,000 (worth more than £2m by
today's standards). Middleton Hall was turned into a home farm.
The estate continued to exchange hands among the wealthy before
Carmarthenshire County Council bought it in the 1930s and turned
it into starter farms. The old mansion was destroyed by fire in
1931. By the 1980s, however, the Middleton farms were too small
to remain viable. The new vision for Middleton came from local
artist William Wilkins, whose aunt had described to him the ruins
of structures she had discovered while walking in the local woods.
Wilkins wanted to create a new botanic garden to represent a

nation, the first for nearly two centuries. Despite many challenges, the garden opened in 2000 – it is now a charity supported by the Welsh Government and Carmarthenshire County Council.

The NBGW is not simply a pleasure garden. It serves important scientific and educational purposes. It includes the British Bird of Prey Centre, Herbarium, Arboretum, Apothecary's Hall and Garden, a children's farm, apiary with beehives and a theatre. Principality House, the former servants' quarters that survived the fire of 1931, is a conference centre. The NBGW is billed as a garden of the future, bringing the arts, humanities and sciences together. The garden is seen as a restored Eden, a place for scientific experimentation and an inspiration for poets and artists.

Ten Amazing Facts about the NBGW

- The garden has plants that smell of toffee, chocolate and curry.
- It also has a few plants that smell of rotting flesh to attract pollinating flies. The smell of the *arum* is so powerful that it drives people out of the Tropical House in the summer.
- There's a wild mushroom called a *cordyceps* that can be found in the nature reserve. This grows out of the body of a caterpillar.
- South African bushmen use the leaves of the quiver tree (found in the Great Glasshouse) to hold their hunting arrows.
- Wales' rarest tree, the Ley's Whitebeam, grows in the NBGW.
- The land train is powered by old chip fat oil.
- The 200-year-old double-walled garden once grew exotic luxury fruit like peaches and pineapples.
- Each of the 785 panes in the glasshouse is a different size. The 147 air vents are computer controlled to regulate the temperature, ensuring it never falls below 9°C.
- Around one million bees visit the bee garden every year.
- Before the invention of fridges, wealthy people used to keep their food fresh and make fruit sorbets with ice stored throughout the year in the icehouse.

Aberglasney

Aberglasney was once billed as 'the garden lost in time' but thanks to the Aberglasney Restoration Trust, some of its former glories have been rediscovered. The restoration of Aberglasney began in earnest during the 1990s and 2000s. Much is once again owed to the energy and determination of local artist and visionary William Wilkins. In 1999 the garden opened to the visiting public, although restoration continues. The most important 'discovery' was the cloister garden dating to the late Tudor and early Stuart years, the best of its kind in the country.

Relatively little is known about the early owners of the house. The first reference is made in 1470 by the poet Lewis Glyn Cothi, who praises Rhdderch ap Rhys for cultivating the land and his nine gardens. Bishop Rudd of St Davids bought and rebuilt the house around 1600. The most famous occupant of the house was the eighteenth-century poet John Dyer. His poem 'Grongar Hill', written in 1726, describes the surrounding area:

> Old castles on the cliffs arise,
> Proudly towering in the skies;
> Rushing from the woods, the spires
> Seem from hence ascending fires;
>
> When will the landscape tire the view!
> The fountain's fall, the river's flow;
> The woody valleys, warm and low;
> The windy summit, wild and high,
> Roughly rushing on the sky;
> The pleasant seat, the ruined tower,
> The naked rock, the shady bower;
> The town and village, dome and farm,
> Each gives each a double charm,
> As pearls upon an Ethiop's arm.

As with most historic houses, Aberglasney has its customary legends and ghost stories. In the 1630s, a housekeeper saw five candles floating around the newly plastered 'blue room'. The next morning, five maidservants were found dead in their beds. The fumes from a charcoal stove, left burning to speed the drying of the plaster, is reputed to have killed them as they slept. The story of the 'corpse candles' became one of Aberglasney's most enduring legends.

In order to maintain the county's gardens and parks as viable concerns, the various owners have diversified to attract visitors by offering art exhibitions, weddings, festivals and concerts.

As the writer Jan Morris points out, when we think of the Welsh cottage of dreams, it does not look like the ideal English cottage bowered in honeysuckle, climbing roses and wisteria. It is more of an austere kind of paradise shaped by a tough, rugged landscape that has no place for wallflowers. This is not to deny the thousands of Welsh gardeners who proudly display their flowerbeds and window boxes. But the true domestic plants of Wales are mosses and ferns, small wild daffodils, wood anemones and yellow poppies. It is no coincidence that the national plant of Wales is not a flower but a kind of onion.

RIVERS, LAKES AND WETLANDS

The county boasts some of the finest rivers in Wales. The two main rivers – the Tywi and Teifi – are well known for their runs of salmon and sewin (sea trout) between April and September. Coracles at Carmarthen once caught sewin weighing more than 20lb. The Teifi offers some 50 miles of fishing along the county's northern border. The smaller rivers Cowin, Cynon and Dewi Fawr have established excellent reputations for trout fishing. Every autumn, sewin make their precarious way upstream to spawn, if they survive the fishermen and women, otter and herons. There are numerous well-stocked fisheries as well as ponds for coarse fishing (carp, perch, trout, roach, bream, pike and tench are the most common fish). The 30 miles or so of beaches provide opportunities for sea fishing. Cefn Sidan and Llanelli North Dock are excellent for bass and flounders.

The Tywi River

The source of the 75-mile-long river is the Cambrian Mountains. The Tywi generally flows south-westwards through the towns of Llandovery, Llandeilo and Carmarthen, where the river mouth joins Carmarthen Bay. The river has always played a major part in the development of these towns. Ships brought exotic goods from

(Library of Congress, LC-DIG-pga-02403)

Gascony and Portugal to Carmarthen Castle and sailed back to mainland Europe with wool, leather, tin and hides. The Tywi is famed for its sea trout (sewin) and salmon.

Coracles

The English word 'coracle' has its origin in the Welsh *cwrwgl*. The coracle has been used as a fishing craft on Carmarthenshire rivers for centuries. The Romans mentioned that the ancient Britons used them. In the 1960s during the fishing season (from mid-April to mid-June), around 400 coracle men operated on the Towy. As of 2019, there were only eight licensed pairs, who fish mostly at night between Carmarthen town and the mouth of the river. The net is held between two coracles, which drift down with the current. The great advantage of coracles is their manoeuvrability over shallow rivers – they only need a few inches of water and can easily nip in between rocks. The fishermen usually carried the 25–30lb coracle on their backs over some distance. The National Coracle Centre at Cenarth includes coracles from the British Isles, North America, India, Tibet and Iraq. The museum is set within a seventeenth-century watermill located beside the beautiful Cenarth Falls. The museum demonstrates techniques of making coracles and tells the history of the ancient practice of poaching. Every August there is a coracle race held downstream at Cilgerran.

Llyn Brianne

The Llyn Brianne reservoir was created in 1972 to store winter rain for release into the river during dry periods, as a kind of 'flow control' for the River Tywi. It then also served as a water supply for the homes and industries of South Wales. The reservoir has a capacity of 14,200 million gallons.

Wetland Centre, Llanelli

This is one of the UK's nine wetland nature reserves managed by the Wildfowl and Wetlands Trust, a nature conservation charity, and the only one in Wales. Visitors enjoy panoramic views over the estuary to see birds that have flown thousands of miles to Llanelli, including glossy ibis, spoonbills, lesser yellowlegs and light-bellied brent geese.

COASTLINE AND BEST BEACHES

In 2014 Carmarthenshire had two beaches awarded the Marine Conservation Society recommendation for clean quality water, featuring on the Good Beach Guide (www.goodbeachguide.co.uk).

Pendine, St Clears

Pendine has a very long sandy, straight beach edged by a belt of sand dunes. From the beach there are clear views across Carmarthen Bay to the Gower and Tenby. This beach is used by the Ministry of Defence and therefore is sometimes closed to the public.

Pembrey

Pembrey has an 8-mile stretch of sand, edged by a belt of sand dunes along the entire length. The beach falls within Pembrey Country Park, which boasts a dry ski slope and the longest toboggan ride in Wales. Visitors can enjoy clear views across Carmarthen Bay to Tenby and the Gower.

WOODLANDS

Woodlands cover about 15 per cent of Carmarthenshire. These are either conifer plantations, introduced since 1940, or native woodland, including oak, ash, beech, sycamore, birch, alder and yew. The plantations cover most of the uplands and make up about 70 per cent of forest, while the native species are scattered around the countryside on land too poor or too difficult to clear for agriculture. The Forestry Commission was set up to manage timber production during the First World War, assuming control of woodland that was no longer productive. This included the ancient Glyn Cothi (Brechfa) Forest, which is wedged between the western edge of the Brecon Beacons National Park and the southern edge of the Cambrian Mountains. It once defended the Welsh principality of Deheubarth. When Edward I defeated the Welsh in 1283, Glyncothi was made a royal forest and people were subject to forest law. This brought severe punishment for anyone cutting trees or caught poaching forest animals such as deer, wild boar, fox and hare. During the seventeenth century, forest law was finally abolished when most of the ancient oaks were felled and cleared. Today, Brechfa Forest covers around 18,000 acres and is managed by the Forestry Commission Wales. Visitors can enjoy stunning walks, mountain bike trails and horse riding. Similar experiences are available at Pembrey, Crychan and Cwm Rhaeadr forests.

8

FOOD AND DRINK

Prior to the Industrial Revolution of the 1800s, most rural Carmarthenshire families lived on what they grew and home-made food, along with what they could find naturally, such as berries on the hedgerows or rabbits on the common. Dairy products such as milk and butter were stored in cellars or even underwater in nearby streams or wells. Food was preserved by methods such as salting, spicing, smoking and pickling. The ability to freeze food changed all of this – the ice revolution and greater use of refrigeration was one of a number of developments that transformed how, when and what people ate and drank.

Carmarthenshire has built up a reputation for beef, lamb, cheese, salmon and beers.

Beef and lamb are among the wide range of products sold at Cwmcerrig Farm, Gorslas (near Cross Hands). Albert Rees Butchers, in Carmarthen market, produce dry-cured 'Carmarthen Ham' by following a recipe that, they claim, dates back to Roman times! According to family legend, the Romans took the recipe with them when they left Carmarthen 1,500 years ago and used it to produce parma ham in Italy. Llandovery market, held at Old Cobbled Market Square, also sells local produce, including cheeses, bread and cakes, butter, chutneys, steam puddings, vegetables, meats and honey. Carmarthen indoor market, which has been selling local produce since 1846, is best visited on Wednesdays and Saturdays.

A small, family-run bakery at Llandysul produces Tregroes Waffles (butter toffee, milk and dark chocolate), which can now be found in all the leading supermarkets in Wales. It began in 1983, when Kees Huysmans took some of his homemade waffles to the local bonfire night celebrations. Today the company produces 4,000 waffles per hour. Perhaps the best way to eat a waffle is to place it on a cup of tea so that the toffee melts to enjoy the full flavour.

Carmarthenshire Cheese Company produces a soft white ripened cheese, Pont Gâr, as well as blue cheese and farmhouse varieties. One of Prince Charles' favourite cheeses – the creamy blue Perl Las (Blue Pearl) – is among those produced at Glyneithinog Farm, Boncath. The cheese-making business began during the 1980s when the family became frustrated over milk quotas. The Royal Family is also partial to Eta Richardson's soft fruitcake at Llansteffan, so much so that it features on the Christmas table at Highgrove.

Resurrection Cheese

In the 1860s, a poor farmer from Llanfihangel Abercywyn could not afford to buy a cheese press. So he crafted a press from fallen headstones taken from the local churchyard. One of the inscriptions, 'In memory of David Thomas', was etched into the circular cheeses. He sold his produce in St Clears market and customers dubbed it Resurrection cheese.

From the end of the nineteenth century to the mid-twentieth century, the region's breweries and other private enterprises produced a variety of soft drinks. These ranged from Felinfoel's Spring Mineral Water to the small-scale grocer Thomas Ferguson, of Victoria Road, Llanelli, who sold home-made ginger beer. By the 1960s they could not compete with the national and multinational companies who had expanded their brands to all parts of the country.

Coles Family Brewers at the White Hart Inn (Llanddarog) brew traditional handcrafted ales, lagers and stouts using a blend of malted barley, hops and water.

PUBS

Throughout its history, Carmarthen seems to have attracted more than its fair share of inns. The oldest known pub (now restaurant), the Angel Vaults, in Nott Square, has a fifteenth-century window, which is all that remains of the church of St Mary, and two narrow medieval lanes, one on each side.

'Ye Nagge's Head' in St Mary's Street was among the first inn to appear in the records of Carmarthen, dating back to 1573. Oliver Cromwell is said to have stayed here during the Civil Wars. By 1802 there were sixty-four inns or alehouses in Carmarthen alone. By then Carmarthen had established itself as a major coaching centre. The Ivy Bush was the most famous of coaching inns, boasting its own railway station.

New Cross, Cwrt Henry
This pub opened in 1909 and consisted of a public bar and a smoking room. The interior has remained remarkably unchanged. Invitations to the opening dinner are preserved in a frame on the mantleshelf.

Cwmdu Inn, Llanedeilo

The community has run the pub and shop since 2000. The building forms part of an early nineteenth-century terrace owned by the National Trust. Annie Griffiths ran the pub and shop for over fifty years, until her death in 1987 at the age of 98. She sold groceries, household items, clothing and a range of miscellaneous goods.

Square and Compass, Llandyfan

The pub is believed to have been built over 300 years ago as a blacksmith's cottage and has been licensed to sell ale since 1840. The symbols of the set-square and compass were used by the Freemasons to represent the body (solid outward appearance) and soul (everlasting creation); however, it is not known whether the Freemasons used the pub as a meeting place.

9

SPORT

Organised sport has been played in Carmarthenshire for centuries. Football and archery, for example, have medieval origins. Today, the county offers everything from aikido (Japanese martial arts) to water sports, cheerleading to croquet, yachting to octopush (underwater hockey) and billiards to basketball. But the county is best known for its rugby.

Rugby

The travel writer Peter Sager said that in England rugby is a game, but in Wales it is a national drug. There is no doubting the passion for the game in Wales, especially when playing against the old enemy. The English public school origins of the game were picked up in the playing fields of Llandovery and Lampeter, where the county's first rugby union teams were formed during the 1850s. The early rugby players were drawn from professionals such as solicitors, teachers and businessmen, but the working classes soon took up the game. Its physical contact and simplicity – a ball, two teams, a playing field and two posts – appealed to the

miners and ironworkers of the South Wales coalfield. Its warrior nature also echoed the old Welsh game of *cnapan*.

Although rugby was well established in the villages and towns throughout Carmarthenshire, Llanelli soon became the county's premier side. John D. Rogers, a pupil at Rugby school where the game began, brought rugby to the town in the 1870s. Despite opposition from chapel ministers, who disliked the contact sport, a team was formed in 1872 and started to play at Stradey Park in 1879. By the 1920s, the team attracted praise for its entertaining, free-flowing style of play. One of their stars, Albert Jenkins, was able to kick a ball the length of the field with either foot. Particularly since the 1960s, Llanelli has produced a string of Welsh captains including Norman Gale, Phil Bennett, Jonathan Davies, Ieuan Evans, Scott Quinnell and Stephen Jones.

Llanelli's heyday was the 1970s. The 'gentle giant' of a captain, Delme Thomas, and the tactical genius of the coach, Carwyn James, led the team to unrivalled success. The finest hour in the history of Llanelli rugby club took place on 31 October 1972 when the Scarlets beat the mighty New Zealand All Blacks 9–3, at Stradey Park, in front of a full house. The triumph was commemorated in comedian and singer Max Boyce's song '9–3'.

Max Boyce's mythical 'Outside Half Factory' is based on the Llanelli district, which has produced Barry John, Carwyn James, Gareth Davies and Jonathan Davies, all born within a 5-mile radius of each other, along with Phil Bennett from the suburb of Felinfoel. Between 1972 and 2000, Llanelli won the Welsh Rugby Union's Challenge Cup a record eleven times. In 2008, Llanelli moved to its new home Parc-y-Scarlets at Pemberton, on the outskirts of the town.

Football

An early form of football called *cnapan* has a long history in West Wales. George Owen, writing in 1603, described how the ancient Britons played the game to improve their strength and stamina. The game involves two sides (sometimes numbering hundreds) from neighbouring parishes attempting to deliver a small wooden ball to a goal, usually the church porch, in their

own parish. The ball was dropped an equal distance from the two goals and the 'pitch' comprised all the land in between. Players were allowed to kick, throw or run with the ball, but this was made more difficult because it was soaked in animal fat the night before. The lack of rules meant that injuries were common and violence often occurred. In 1838, local magistrates in Laugharne suppressed the game because they saw it as a public nuisance.

From the 1850s, Llandovery public school masters, along with other masters educated in England, introduced versions of football to their scholars. For the middle classes, football and rugby offered a means of keeping the workforces content and peaceful while building up a sense of identity. This was especially so in the heavily industrialised centres such as Llanelli. In the 1890s, men from Staffordshire brought the game to Llanelli when they came to work in the pottery industry. A Geordie, Jack Harding, who had previously played in the Wearside League, established a Carmarthen team in 1920. Carmarthen Town Association Football Club (AFC) was formed in 1950 and plays its home games in the Welsh Premier League at Richmond Park, watched by crowds of around 300. Sadly, Llanelli AFC, formed in 1896, was wound up in 2013 following financial problems. However, it was soon reborn and has enjoyed considerable success at Welsh League level.

Other Sports

Carmarthenshire has a range of other well-established sports. Cricket is the oldest team game in Wales and was introduced to Carmarthenshire in the late eighteenth century. The Carmarthenshire Lawn Tennis and Archery Club first met in Llandeilo in 1884, although an archery club was practicing in the 1860s. Archery was the only sport women enjoyed prior to the nineteenth century. Golf has been played at Ashburnham, in Burry Port, since the 1890s, while golf clubs were established at Carmarthen and Glynhir by the 1900s. The course at Machynis opened in 2005 and has hosted Welsh Ryder Cups. Under the direction of Augustus Brigstocke and other well-to-do figures, a hockey club was formed in Newcastle Emlyn in 1896 with the intention of playing the game 'in its most modern and scientific form'. Youngsters in Carmarthen streets were soon reported to be engaging madly in the game with old walking sticks and a ball. Carmarthen and Landovery County Girls Schools were among the early pacesetters.

Cycling became even more popular and something of a national craze in the 1890s. It offered newfound freedoms for girls and young ladies, although onlookers expressed concern over the speed and daring nature of the cyclists. In 1901, David Davies from Pontyberem was fined 5s and sent to prison for fourteen days for unlawfully riding a bicycle 'furiously so as to endanger the life and limb of any passenger on the highway'. He was also ordered to pay 9s 7d compensation to the local policeman! By the 1900s, accidents and bicycle thefts were common but provide indications of how popular the sport had become. Carmarthen Park's cycle track, which opened in 1900, was said to rival any in England and Wales.

In athletics, Carmarthen and District Harriers were formed in 1948 and by the 1960s, top British sprinters were participating in road races held in Carmarthen. Many Welsh championships and international races have been held at the Carmarthen Athletics Track. By the 1830s, horse racing had been arranged at Llanboidy. In more recent times, the Ffos Las racecourse (meaning, 'blue ditch', and named after the farm that occupied the site) was built on the site of an old opencast mine. Its first race was held in 2009 and was the first new National Hunt racecourse to be built in the UK for eighty years.

'Blood sports' such as fox and otter hunting have long been associated with Carmarthenshire rural life. In the 1900s, Carmarthenshire Hunt Week was a highlight in the social calendar of the wealthy, culminating in the Hunt Ball at the Assembly Rooms in Carmarthen. The working classes enjoyed gambling on violent pastimes such as fist fighting, badger baiting and cockfighting, the latter introduced by the Romans. Men called 'feeders' trained the birds over many months. In 1849, cockfighting was made illegal to protect the birds and to stop the gathering of unruly crowds. The village of Croesyceiliog ('Cockerel's Cross') may have derived its name from cockfighting.

10

INDUSTRY AND
THE ENVIRONMENT

Today the major employers in the county are Carmarthenshire
County Council, Dyfed Powys Police and the education sector.
Historically, most people earned a living as farmers, labourers
and domestic servants. In 1911, around one in five of the county's
53,000 workers were employed in agriculture. This proportion
steadily declined during the twentieth century, reaching around
one in nine by 1971. With the industrialisation of the county,
many worked in the coal, tinplate and communication (rail, road
and sea) industries. By the nineteenth century, the county had
come to consist of two distinct areas: the agricultural district
around Carmarthen and the anthracite coalfield based in the
Amman and Gwendraeth valleys. Geographical factors, such
as the large number of streams and temperate climate, meant
that many of the industrial villages retained their rural roots.
In contrast to the mining communities in the Rhondda Valley,
farms worked alongside the pits in the Gwendraeth villages.
This contributed to the preservation of the Welsh language and
culture in these communities.

AGRICULTURE

Traditionally, the pattern of farming in the county was mixed:
arable, pastoral and dairy. Arable farming included oats, barley
and, to a lesser extent, wheat, along with vegetable crops such as
potatoes, peas and turnips. Farmers used mainly lime as a fertiliser
to neutralise the acidic soil. Hence various limekilns were set up

across the county – six kilns opened around Llandybïe in 1856, increasing to nine by 1900, capable of producing 20 tons of lime per day. Farmers had to pay a daily toll to collect the lime and so during the summer months a long line of horses would assemble at midnight for the journey to the kilns, hoping to complete the trip within twenty-four hours to avoid paying a second fee.

Carmarthenshire's pastoral farming was based on sheep, cattle and horses. Sheep were reared mainly in the upland areas in the north and north east of the county. The farming heritage is preserved in various shows. The oldest is the Cothi Bridge Show (started in 1898), run by the Welsh Pony and Cob Society. In the summer there are shows at Bancffosfelen, Cwmdu and Trap, while the Llandyfaelog show is held in September.

In the nineteenth century, the coming of the railway network transformed agriculture. It meant that farmers had new markets for dairy produce and poultry and it led to the gradual introduction of agricultural machinery and imported foods. Agricultural societies and landowners promoted ploughing competitions among farmers to spur on improvements. At Llandovery in 1844, the winning prize was a 'new suit of clothes' while all those who entered the competition in Llanelli in 1855 were promised a free dinner. These competitions became major social events, which extended into the evening, attracting criticisms from chapel ministers over the drinking of alcohol. During the First World War special classes were extended to women. The competitions only declined in the 1920s when there was a significant shift away from arable towards dairy farming. However, they resurfaced with the growth of Young Farmers' Clubs in the late 1940s, although they were restricted to tractor ploughing.

Most of the farmers in the Tywi Valley and the area bordering the railway line from Carmarthen westwards became almost exclusively dairy farms. Although dairy farming remains important in Carmarthenshire and Wales, accounting for around 27 per cent of farm output, the dairy industry has suffered in the past decade. In particular, small family-run Carmarthenshire farms struggle to survive. The farmers have seen their milk profits squeezed by supermarkets and processing plants, so much so that milk is said to be cheaper than water. The closure of the last creamery in the county was a further blow. Dairy Crest had originally closed its Whitland plant in 1994 but it was relaunched in 2011 in an effort to keep Welsh milk bottled in Wales. In 2014, however, it was forced to close because further investment was needed to maintain the shelf life for milk demanded by supermarkets. Milk from 122 dairy farms is now transported for processing in Stroud, Gloucestershire to be returned to Wales in bottles.

Over the past few decades the farming industry has experienced a number of challenges, including a severe outbreak of foot and mouth disease in 2001, and farmers have had to diversify into areas such as tourism and organic farming.

COAL

There is a long history of coal mining in Carmarthenshire. John Leland, who travelled around Wales in the 1530s, pointed out 'Ther lieth a long on eche side of Wendraeth Vaur Pittes, wher menne digge se cole.' By the eighteenth century, the county's major landowning families tapped the natural resources by opening pits around Llanelli. There were over 1,000 employed in the area in 1841, including women and children. By 1907 the number of Llanelli miners alone reached 1,500. The demand for coal was partly triggered by the increasing use of steamships and steam engines.

Children had been employed in the Carmarthenshire pits since they first opened. They worked mainly as 'trappers', opening and shutting doors to allow trams to pass through. The youngest boys were 5 to 6 year olds who began their 12-hour shifts at 6 a.m. Girls worked on the surface, picking slates and stones from the coal on the banks at the pit top. The children brought a bag of bread and cheese to eat during the day, and returned to their homes in the same clothes, sometimes wet through. Accidents were common, sometimes because children fell asleep. Two Llanelli doctors told an 1842 government inquiry into the employment of children underground that children were often sickly in appearance and many maimed for life.

Coal could be exported quickly via the coast. As the easier and shallower seams were fully exploited, entrepreneurs and industrialists such as Alexander Raby brought investment through specialised steam engines and pumps. The coal industry was responsible for the creation of villages around the mines, including Penygroes, Cross Hands, Tumble, Cwmmawr, Pontyberem, Ponthenry and Trimsaran. In the area of Trimsaran alone, there were forty collieries. The most significant pit was the Great Mountain Colliery in Tumble, which opened in 1887. By 1913 it employed 837 men. The rows of houses in and around Tumble High Street were built for the employees and the building legacy is also evident in workingmen's institutes and pubs to be found in the former mining villages.

The South Wales coalfield extends to the south-east corner of the county, with the River Gwendraeth Fawr marking its western boundary. The high carbon content of the county's anthracite coal makes it ideal for domestic consumption because it gives off very little smoke and burns with intense heat. The superior qualities of anthracite were soon recognised – exports rose from 80,000 tons in 1886 to more than 1.2 million by 1911. In the 1900s, new collieries opened each year across the Gwendraeth and Amman valleys. Legend has it that local developers tasted the soil to know where to sink the pits. The heyday of anthracite production was in the 1930s and '40s – over 6 million tons were produced in 1934 alone. By 1940, there were eight collieries in the Gwendraeth Valley with an output of half a million tons per year.

The Gwendraeth Valley did not attract the same levels of migration from England and Ireland as other valleys in the South Wales coalfield. As a result, Welsh-speaking culture remained strong.

Coal mining was a dangerous business. Between 1853 and 1974, around 24,000 Welsh miners were killed in the pits – 429 died in the 1960s. Miners worked under difficult conditions on their

backs in narrow seams. Methane gas or firedamp was usually released from the coal seams into the atmosphere. Effective ventilation became essential in the deeper mines and so two shafts were sunk, one to extract foul air and the other to allow fresh air to enter. Explosions of methane gas, roof falls, inrushing water and runaway mine carts were all common problems. The spontaneous outbursts of coal dust and methane gas under high pressure was known as 'blowers' and this was the cause of the worse mining disaster in Carmarthenshire history. On 10 May 1852, twenty-six men were killed at Pontyberem. The youngest victim was 13-year-old John Harris. The only survivor, David Evans, described how a vast body of water overwhelmed the colliers as they tried to climb into a cage to escape to the surface. He lost grip of one boy, who drowned with his companions. A memorial to the victims can be seen in the centre of the village. Local historian Phil Cumin has calculated that a further 226 outbursts of coal and methane gas occurred in the Gwendraeth Valley in the period 1913–85, claiming an additional twenty-seven lives.

Major Carmarthenshire Pit Disasters

Date	Location	Fatalities
6 July 1840	St Davids Pit, Llangennech	five
10 May 1852	Gwendraeth (Watney), Pontyberem	twenty-six
3 July 1862	Old Castle, Llanelli	six
26 April 1923	Trimsaran	ten
3 September 1924	Ponthenry, Llanelli	five
6 September 1955	Blaenhirwaun, Cross Hands	five

The ten men at Trimsaran lost their lives in 1923 when the link in the carriages they were travelling in snapped, sending the miners and their tools hurling down a 1,400yd slope. The youngest victim was 16-year-old Harold Probert. Although the large explosions made the newspaper headlines, these were not the major cause of death underground. Roof-falls tended to kill one or two miners at a time and escaped major publicity. The operation of the cage, which carried men and materials up and down the shaft, was also a dangerous business. Another factor that contributed to the high incidence of accidents was that miners were paid by piecework, depending upon the amount of coal produced. This meant that miners cut corners on safety. It was not until the setting up of the National Coal Board in 1947 and the nationalisation of the industry that miners were paid a fixed wage. In the 1930s, the Waddle engineering company in Llanelli created a giant fan (20ft in diameter), which was placed at the head of coalmines to draw air through the shafts. Such inventions saved many thousands of coal miners' lives.

The coal industry declined significantly after the Second World War. There were regular closures in each decade: Pontyberem (1949), Saron (1956), Great Mountain (1962), Ammanford (1976), Cynheidre (1989) and Betws (1992/93), to name a few. Ammanford Colliery was the last deep mine in Wales to bring coal to the surface by rope-hauled trams.

Bitterness remains in many households over the government's handling of the miners' strike (1984-85) and the running down of the coal industry on the grounds that it was unprofitable. It is claimed that British Coal deliberately presented Betws Colliery in a negative light, forcing it to sell coal to its marketing company at less than market prices, while the marketing company then sold directly to the customers at the going rate. Thus one view is that Betws Colliery was set up to make a loss for political reasons, so that public funds could be directed into alternative energy sources such as nuclear power and gas.

IRON

As early as 1611, there was an ironworks in the village of Ponthenri using local iron-ore supplies from Mynydd-y-garreg. In western Carmarthenshire, a forge at Whitland supplied ammunition for Oliver Cromwell's attack on Pembroke Castle during the Civil War in the 1640s. By the early 1700s, ironworks had also been established at Cwmbran (near Cynwyl Elfed), Cwmdwyfran, Llandyfan and Kidwelly. To function well, forges needed a regular water supply and access to cheap charcoal. A waterwheel provided power for the bellows and the tilt hammers. This meant that the forge or furnace had to be located on or near the banks of a swiftly running stream which provided a constant and regular flow of water throughout the year. Charcoal was used in the smelting and refining processes so, to keep transport costs low, the ironmasters set up their works near woodlands.

Robert Morgan, one of the leading ironmasters in eighteenth-century Carmarthenshire, lived in Furnace House in St Peter's Street, Carmarthen, which is now the county library. Many of the railings surrounding chapels and schools are testimony to the town's iron heritage. Morgan increased production at his Kidwelly ironworks from 100 to 400 tons between 1750 and 1788.

His most important contribution to the industrial development of the county, however, was the upgrading of his works to produce steel and tinplate. Steel is a stronger metal than iron and offers more durability. By the 1840s and '50s, new ironworks at Dafen and Morfa concentrated on the production of tinplate. In the early 1900s, steelworks opened in Llanelli.

TINPLATE

The South Wales tinplate industry developed from the iron and steel industries. The industry centred on Llanelli, Kidwelly and Swansea because of ready access to the raw materials – coal, iron and water. Tinplate involved flattening and rolling iron plates and coating them with tin. It was a complex process, demanding considerable strength and skill. In 1737, Charles Gwynn of Kidwelly established the first tinworks in the county. It was located at Bank Broadford in the valley of the Gwendraeth Fach, about a mile to the north of Kidwelly. The town had been a port since medieval times and was well located for the import of tin from Cornwall and the 'tough iron' from South and West Wales, which was needed for the production of tinplate.

In 1809 a French chef called Nicholas Appert came up with the idea of preserving and sterilising fruit by boiling it in sealed glass containers. The seal remained intact until the fruit was ready to eat. In England, the idea was extended to using tin canisters, which were less likely to break than glass. Samples of boiled beef were sent to military leaders, including the Duke of Wellington, who were impressed by the taste. In 1958, a can of meat recovered from a polar expedition of 1824 was found to be still in a good state! Businessmen could see the potential market and the American canning industry demanded British tinplate. Tinplate production thus rose from 4,000 tons in 1805 to 586,000 tons by 1890. The Carmarthenshire tinplate works were very much at the centre of this trade.

Working in the tinplate industry was very tough. A survey in 1901 reported that the average age at death of a tinplate man in South Wales was 32. Another survey in 1912 was more optimistic, but at 45 years this was still well below the average lifespan of farmers (67), gardeners (68) and even coalminers (51). Children easily cut themselves when handling the sharp corners of tinplate sheets.

To the modern reader, workers in the industry undertook all kinds of strange-sounding jobs. These included 'behinders' who caught sheets of tinplate and passed them back to the 'rollerman'. There were 'boxers', 'melters', 'picklers', 'risers', 'shinglers' and 'washmen'. By 1881 the tinplate industry was third as a provider of employment in Carmarthenshire (agriculture and domestic service being first and second).

The decline of the tinplate industry during the 1890s was triggered by international competition. The American Congress passed legislation in 1890, following campaigning by William McKinley (later Governor of Ohio), which sought to protect the emerging American tinplate industry by imposing tariffs on imported tinplate. To remain competitive, British companies had to reduce prices and struggled to make profits. From 1896 to 1999, thirty-six tinplate works closed in South Wales, including Kidwelly, leaving 150 families in destitution, reliant upon soup kitchens and charitable donations. In the 1900s, exploration of new markets and the expansion of the food canning industry went some way to resurrect the tinplate trade.

Llanelli's tinplate heritage is reflected in the famous Welsh folk song, 'Sospan Fach' ('Little Saucepan'). The industry mass-produced steel saucepans and other kitchen utensils for the public. Saucepans adorn rugby posts upon entering the town near the club's ground at Pemberton.

Sospan Fach

Welsh	English (literal translation)
Mae bys Meri-Ann wedi brifo,	Mary-Ann has hurt her finger,
A Dafydd y gwas ddim yn iach.	And David the servant is not well.
Mae'r baban yn y crud yn crio,	The baby in the cradle is crying,
A'r gath wedi sgrapo Joni bach.	And the cat has scratched little Johnny.
Sosban fach yn berwi ar y tân,	A little saucepan is boiling on the fire,
Sosban fawr yn berwi ar y llawr,	A big saucepan is boiling on the floor,
A'r gath wedi sgrapo Joni bach.	And the cat has scratched little Johnny.
Dai bach y sowldiwr,	Little Dai the soldier,
Dai bach y sowldiwr,	Little Dai the soldier,
Dai bach y sowldiwr,	Little Dai the soldier,
A gwt ei grys e mas.	And his shirt tail is hanging out.
Mae bys Meri-Ann wedi gwella,	Mary-Ann's finger has got better,
A Dafydd y gwas yn ei fedd;	And David the servant is in his grave;
Mae'r baban yn y crud wedi tyfu,	The baby in the cradle has grown up,
A'r gath wedi huno mewn hedd.	And the cat is 'asleep in peace'.
Sosban fach yn berwi ar y tân	A little saucepan is boiling on the fire,
Sosban fawr yn berwi ar y llawr	A big saucepan is boiling on the floor,
A'r gath wedi huno mewn hedd.	And the cat is 'asleep in peace'.
Dai bach y sowldiwr,	Little Dai the soldier,
Dai bach y sowldiwr,	Little Dai the soldier,
Dai bach y sowldiwr,	Little Dai the soldier,
A gwt ei grys e mas.	And his shirt tail is hanging out.
Aeth hen Fari Jones i Ffair y Caerau	Old Mary Jones went to the fair in Caerau,
I brynu set o lestri de;	To buy a tea set;
Ond mynd i'r ffos aeth Mari gyda'i llestri	But Mary and her teacups ended up in a ditch,
Trwy yfed gormod lawer iawn o 'de'	Through the consumption of rather too much 'tea'.
Sosban fach yn berwi ar y tân	A little saucepan is boiling on the fire,
Sosban fawr yn berwi ar y llawr	A big saucepan is boiling on the floor,
A'r gath wedi huno mewn hedd.	And the cat is 'asleep in peace'.

COPPER

Life today would be very different if it were not for the copper industry. Everything from coins to telephones depends upon copper. The Royal Navy relied upon its copper-bottomed ships, which made them more manoeuvrable in battles such as Trafalgar.

The copper-smelting industry was linked to the growth of the coal industry. By the early nineteenth century, Swansea had established itself as Britain's leading centre for copper production – it was known as 'Copperopolis'. The Nevill family founded the Llanelly Copperworks Company in 1805. Boys as young as 8 years old were routinely employed; they worked with their fathers from 6 a.m. and remained until about 8 p.m. The youngest boys were generally paid 6s to 8s per week, while the oldest boys received up to 14s per week. There was no shortage of boys willing to take up the offer of employment. Two local surgeons were of the view that:

> The custom of subsisting on dry food [bread and cheese] for eight to ten hours during the time of work, together with the inhalation of an impure atmosphere cannot otherwise, in our opinion, than operate in producing the results above described [smallness of stature and a sickly appearance].

The employers provided primary education through the Llanelli Copperworks School.

By the 1900s the Welsh copper industry had declined in the face of foreign competition. New smelting centres were set up nearer to the sources of copper ore, particularly in North and South America, South Africa and Australia, which drew men from Wales.

LEAD

Carmarthenshire was once home to a dozen or more lead mines. The largest operated in the northern parts of the Tywi Valley. At Nant-y-mwym mine in the 1780s, around 400 men were employed to produce around 1,200 tons of ore. The mine continued working until the early 1930s, by which time it was no longer cost effective.

MUNITIONS

There has been a factory making gunpowder in Pembrey since 1881. During the 1880s and '90s, explosives were taken by horse-drawn transport from Pembrey works via Carmarthen, to the slate quarries (Portmadoc and Blaenau Ffestiniog) of North Wales, where the explosives were used. By nature, working in a munitions factory was a dangerous business. In November 1918 Mary Fitzmaurice, a mother of seven children, died along with two other women trying to disassemble shells brought back from France following the end of the war. History repeated itself after the Second World War when several men died at the Burry Port Royal Ordnance Factory while clearing explosives from the shells, to make steel available to sell as scrap.

WOOL

For generations, sheep farming and the wool industry provided a livelihood for many families in Carmarthenshire. Every community had its spinners, weavers and stocking knitters supplying local needs. The heyday of the wool industry was between 1880 and 1918 and was centred in the Teifi Valley with its fast-flowing streams. The National Wool Museum at Dre-fach Felindre is housed in the old Cambrian Mills, once the centre of the then flourishing Welsh wool industry. The museum tells the story of an industry that produced blankets and bedcovers, shirts and shawls, and woollen stockings, sold both in local markets and all over the world. The villages of Cwmpengraig and Cwmhiraeth were known as 'the Huddersfield of Wales'.

It was the custom in West Wales for poor women to 'harvest' discarded wool from hedgerows and mountains. They would bring along sacks to gather the wool and small provisions to sustain a group for a week or so. Hillside farmers granted them permission to wander and often exchanged services – accommodation for assistance

Welsh spinners (Library of Congress, LC-DIG-ppmsc-07502)

around the farm. The gatherers welcomed a warm spring because it meant that the sheep were more likely to shed their wool freely.

Colliers in the Gwendraeth Valley needed flannel shirts, socks and undergarments. Employees were paid in both money and goods, such as blankets, skirts or suits. Many men, women and children worked on the farm as well as in the mill. In the 1900s, children of school age worked from 5 p.m. until 8 p.m., for which they were paid 3*d*. By then, over 1,000 people worked in the twenty or so woollen mills. Many of the houses in the area, which today are sought after by holidaymakers, were originally built for mill workers.

By the 1920s the wool industry was in decline, suffering from poor management, a lack of investment and foreign competition.

MARITIME

Carmarthenshire has a very long maritime history. The first prehistoric settlers depended upon local rivers to supply them with fish, while a succession of invaders, from the Romans to the Normans, built their major settlements in close proximity to the sea. Carmarthen and Laugharne developed as important medieval ports and Tudor merchants brought in spices and goods to Carmarthen, following the expansion of the sea routes. By the 1830s, new harbours opened at Pembrey and Burry Port, contributing to the industrialisation of the county. Coal and tin was shipped all over the world.

Seafaring was very much a young man's pursuit. Nineteenth-century government inspectors supported the setting up of navigation schools such as the one run by Captain Phillips at Seaside in Llanelli, where young men could study to gain certificates to become masters. A 14-year-old apprentice might earn 10*s* a month in the 1840s, an ordinary seaman would get £1–£2 a month, and an able seaman could earn £2 5*s* a month. A master could earn as much as £8 per month. Much depended on the size of the vessel and the nature of the voyage. Most of the crews who manned the Llanelli and Burry Port ships were Welsh speakers, and sons often followed their fathers to sea. However, competition for work in the tinplate industry meant a shortage of local mates by the end of the century. Increasingly by the 1900s, masters were relying on foreign crews who were said to be 'more pliable, more amenable to duty, more sober' but after three years serving on a British ship they were reported to be 'not so good'.

Cockle fishing has been practiced since ancient times in Carmarthen Bay, especially in the Burry inlet. The demand for shellfish and other cheap food increased with the population expansion in the nineteenth century. At its peak, it was estimated that 500 families earned a living gathering cockles at Ferryside, Penclawdd and elsewhere around Llanelli; the value of the stock was more than £15,000 a year in 1850 (over £850,000 today).

Cockle gathering declined for many reasons, ranging from pollution, the ferocious appetite of oystercatchers (one study in 1961–62 revealed that, over three months, they ate 6 million cockles in the Bury inlet), possible cockle migration, overfishing, mystery bugs and changes to the course of the River Loughor. The most recent government inquiry in 2012 found that pollution was not to blame, but locals were not convinced.

OTHER INDUSTRIES

For centuries, many Carmarthenshire people earned a living through small cottage industries such as spinning and weaving. The Industrial Revolution spawned many minor industries including the manufacture of soap, salt, glass and various chemicals. After 1850, there were four chemical works in Llanelli manufacturing vitriol, mainly for the local tinplate works. There were several brickworks within the county, each bearing their names on the bricks, including Brynamman, Carmarthen, Dafen, Llangennech and Trimsaran. Many walkers continue to find engraved bricks, reminders of a once thriving industry. The South Wales Pottery (1839–1920) was situated on the present site of the Asda supermarket in Llanelli, commemorated by a blue plaque and heritage panel. Workers built the row of cottages in Pottery Street, sharing their resources in an early form of building society. Each item of pottery bore the mark SWP. Examples of products can be viewed at the town's Parc Howard Museum.

SELECT
BIBLIOGRAPHY

If you want to gain an in-depth knowledge of the county's history, then the best reference work remains the two-volume *History of Carmarthenshire* (1939) edited by Sir John Edward Lloyd. But this was published more than seventy years ago. Since then, A.G. Prys Jones, a former pupil at Llandovery College and later school inspector, retold the story of Carmarthenshire in his two volumes during the 1970s. More recently, Dylan Rees has written a concise guide to the county in a series for the University of Wales Press, and there are many fascinating local histories of the county's villages generously sponsored by the local authority. These are all available in the county library in Carmarthen.

The growing interest in local and family history, coupled with ready access via the Internet, has added much to our understanding of Carmarthenshire's rich heritage. Well-informed articles in *The Carmarthenshire Antiquary* (published since 1905) offer insight into everything from Bronze Age monuments in the Gwendraeth Valley to 'Admiral Nelson Slept Here', from a survey of medieval fishponds at Whitland Abbey to a summer in Llansteffan in 1879, from the Carmarthenshire butter trade to the diary of an Eton schoolboy visiting the Amman Valley in 1843. There are now publications on most aspects of the county's past, from the Carmarthen Pals of the First World War to rugby tales at Stradey Park.

One very good starting point is the Discover Carmarthenshire website, which provides excellent guides to local walks: www.discovercarmarthenshire.com

BOOKS

Cullen, P., *Outburst: Curse Below the Gwendraeth Valley* (Carmarthen: Carmarthenshire County Council, 2001)

Dames, M., *Merlin and Wales: A Magician's Landscape* (London: Thames and Hudson, 2002).

David, P., *A Garden Lost in Time: Mystery of the Ancient Gardens of Aberglasney* (London: Weidenfeld & Nicolson, 1999)

Davies, G., *Carmarthenshire Villages* (Ammanford: Sigma, 2012)

Davies, R. *Secret Sins: Sex, Violence and Society in Carmarthenshire 1870-1920* (Cardiff: University of Wales Press, 2012).

Davis, P., *Historic West Wales* (Swansea: Christopher Davies, 1992)

Day, K., *Beloved Tywi* (Llandysul: Gomer, 2006)

Edwards, J., *Remembrance of a Riot: The Story of the Llanelli Railway Strike Riots of 1911* (1988)

Edwards, J., *Llanelli: Story of a Town* (Derby: DB Publishing, 2013)

Gower, J., *The Real Llanelli* (Bridgend: Seren, 2009)

Grigg. R., *History of Trinity College Carmarthen* (Cardiff: University of Wales Press, 1998)

Hughes, W., *Carmarthen: A History and Celebration of the Town* (Salisbury: Frith Book Company, 2004)

Jenkins, J.G., *The Coracle,* Welsh Crafts series (Conwy: Gwasg Carreg Gwalch, 2007)

Jones, F., *Historic Carmarthenshire Homes and their Families* (Carmarthen: Carmarthenshire Antiquarian Society, 1987)

Lloyd, Sir J.E., *History of Carmarthenshire*, vol. 1 (Cardiff: London Carmarthenshire Society, 1935)

Lloyd, Sir J.E., *History of Carmarthenshire*, vol. 2 (Cardiff: London Carmarthenshire Society, 1939)

Lodwick, J. and V., *The Story of Carmarthen* (Carmarthen: St Peters Press, 1994)

Molloy, P., *A Shilling for Carmarthen* (Llandysul: Gwasg Gomer, 1980)

Molloy, P., *And They Blessed Rebecca* (Llandysul: Gwasg Gomer, 1983)

Owen, T.M., *The Customs and Traditions of Wales* (Cardiff: University of Wales Press, 2006)

Rees, D., *Carmarthenshire: The Concise History* (Cardiff: University of Wales Press, 2005)

Sclater, A., *The National Botanic Garden of Wales* (London: HarperCollins, 2000)

Spurrell, W., *Carmarthen and its Neighbourhood* (Carmarthen: Dyfed Cultural Services, 1995 reprint)

WEBSITES

Carmarthen Gaol photographs, www.welshlegalhistory.org/carms-felons-register.php

Carmarthen workhouses, www.workhouses.org.uk

Carmarthenshire beaches, www.goodbeachguide.co.uk

Discover Carmarthenshire, www.discovercarmarthenshire.com

Kidwelly history, www.kidwellyhistory.co.uk/contents htm

Lichfield (Llandeilo Fawr) Gospels, https://lichfield.as.uky.edu

Llandeilo Org, www.llandeilo.org/index.php

Llanelli Community Heritage, www.llanellich.org.uk

The Gate art and craft gallery, www.the-gate.org

West Wales Memorial website, www.wwwmp.co.uk